CRAVE EAT HEAL

Front Table Books • An imprint of Cedar Fort, Inc. • Springville, Utah

Annie Oliverio

CRAVE EAT HEAL

plant-based whole food recipes to satisfy every appetite

ISBN 13: 978-1-4621-1555-6

Published by Front Table Books, an imprint of Cedar Fort, Inc.
2373 W. 700 S., Springville, UT 84663
Distributed by Cedar Fort, Inc. www.cedarfort.com

Library of Congress Control Number: 2014957685

Cover design by Bekah Claussen and Lauren Error
Cover design © 2015 Lyle Mortimer
Edited by Hannah Ballard and Justin Greer

Printed in China

10 9 8 7 6 5 4 3 2 1

To Ike, whose tail-wags, wet kisses, melodious yawns, and joyful running remind me that veganism is not about ingredients. It's about the animals.

To Kel, whose palate I most like to please.

And to my Vitamix Turboblend VS for taking all of the cashews, almonds, kale, nutritional yeast, tofu, bananas, and frozen pineapple I can throw at it and responding, "Is that all you've got?!"

"*Crave Eat Heal* is an innovative cookbook designed to help you satisfy your food cravings while enjoying delicious plant-based recipes. Organized according to craving, from creamy, comfort, and chocolate to salty, sweet, and spicy, these recipes and accompanying photographs are a feast for all the senses."
—Robin Robertson, bestselling author of *Vegan Without Borders, Vegan Planet, One-Dish Vegan*, and many more

"Annie Oliverio proves that a healthy, plant-based diet can satisfy your every craving: healthfully, deliciously, and completely without guilt. If you think that eating healthy means giving up treats that are sweet, salty, creamy, or otherwise comforting, you've really got a treat in store for you in *Crave Eat Heal*."
— Nava Atlas, author of *Plant Power* and *Wild About Greens*

"You know how sometimes you'd like to just grab a book off the shelf to find the exact right food to satisfy a craving? And you want it to be vegan? Now you can! *Crave Eat Heal*, cleverly laid out by craving type, is packed with recipes that will please long-time vegans and just may push the veg-curious over into the world of plant-based eating. Filled with whole foods recipes that are good for you—but more importantly plain good—there is something for everyone."
—JL Fields, vegan cook, coach, and consultant, and author of *Vegan Pressure Cooking: Beans, Grains, and One-Pot Meals in Minutes* and coauthor of *Vegan for Her: The Woman's Guide to Being Healthy and Fit on a Plant-Based Diet*

TABLE OF CONTENTS

INTRODUCTION

Cravings

I know a little something about cravings. I was the kid who curled up on the couch with a book and a stash of Jolly Rancher candies, a pack of bubble gum, and a few chocolate Kisses "just in case." I was the young adult whose dinner was often a bag of buttery microwave popcorn followed by a pint of double chocolate chip ice cream; and I was the adult who, without fail, rewarded herself after her daily workout with a bag of M&M'S or a Twix bar.

As you can see, my cravings tended toward the sugary variety, but cravings come in all varieties: salty, sweet, tart, spicy, and so on. After many years of guilty feelings about my intense food desires, I realize that cravings are my body's way of telling me it needs something: more water, healthy fat, stress-relief, comfort, or exercise. But now instead of reaching for sugar-heavy, processed candy, I treat my body to nutrient-rich, plant-based whole foods.

In this book, I give you recipes that will satisfy your own forbidden food desires with healthy, whole food, plant-based recipes that cover the spectrum from sweet to savory. And—bonus!—these recipes include foods that do double duty. While they are taming your sweet (or your salty, tangy, spicy) tooth, ingredients like ginger, chia, cacao, garlic, greens, nuts, seeds, spices, and citrus will provide your body with the complex vitamins and minerals that it needs to heal, to grow, and to function at its best.

My Food History & Philosophy

Like many women, I have a complex and troubled past with food. I was a slightly picky toddler whose tastes gravitated toward the sweet, coupled with an obsession with peanuts and peanut butter. As a teenager, I got into the bad habit of depriving myself of food for most of the day. The thought of breakfast made me nauseated, and at lunchtime at school, even though ravenous, I usually turned up my nose at the sandwich and fruit my mother packed for me to eat. I did, however, always eat the cookies. Then I'd get home from school and grab a bag of chips or dip a big spoon straight into a jar of Jif. By the time dinner rolled around, I was a cranky, starving mess! Needless to say, this is a terrible way to treat a growing body.

Once I was on my own and responsible for stocking my own shelves and refrigerator, I would load up on boxed macaroni and cheese, salty crackers, cookies, and processed baked goods. When I wanted to treat myself, I bought a cheese- and chili-covered Coney dog and followed that with a handful of Oreo cookies. Coca-Cola was my beverage of choice.

This "diet" seemed to have no ill effect on me (aside from the sugar highs and lows I inevitably experienced throughout the day) until I neared thirty. That's when I realized that if I didn't change my habits, I could kiss my slim figure goodbye; it didn't cross my mind that I was also setting myself up for heart disease, high blood pressure, and Type II diabetes.

Spurred on by my expanding waistline, I made small—very small—changes over a long period of time. I'm talking years. First, I started jogging. I hated every painful step, but I stuck to it, and now can't imagine life without it. The better running made me feel, the more I sought out other ways to improve my health. I added strength training, yoga, and Pilates to my routine. This led to making small changes in my dietary choices; it's almost inevitable that one healthy habit leads to another.

Books and movies led me to make bigger changes. After watching *Super Size Me*, I went cold turkey on fast food. Then, I gave up refined sugars. Meanwhile, I began reading about nutrition and the role that food plays in how our bodies function. After reading *Fast Food Nation* by Eric Schlosser, I again went cold turkey—this time on turkey and all meats. I wasn't quite ready to kick my good friends, cheese and fish, to the curb, however.

Then in 2010, my brother learned that he had terminal brain cancer. That's when my research into food and nutrition went into overdrive. I was hoping to find a way to positively impact his treatment, tame the side effects of the chemotherapy, and slow down the progress of his disease. To better understand the connection between consuming animal products and cancer, I read *The China Study* by T. Colin Campbell, and afterwards said goodbye forever to fish, seafood, and dairy. So long yogurt, milk, cheese, shrimp, and salmon. At the same time, I severely curbed my intake of oils and processed fats. I learned that the key to disease prevention comes from what we put into our bodies. Plants are packed with powerful phytonutrients that work with our bodies own defenses to protect and heal. Unfortunately, this wisdom came far too late for me to help my brother, but for many of us, it's not too late. It's not too late to reverse the damage we've done to ourselves through our food choices, to prevent future ailments, and to provide our bodies with what it needs to function pain- and illness-free.

At its most fundamental, food is what fuels our minds and bodies, but its most important role is that of uniting and bringing family, friends, and sometimes strangers together. We plan our holidays and celebrations around what we are going to eat. Food encourages conversation, sharing, and love. And in the case of vegans, it sometimes sparks philosophical debates and heated arguments and causes bruised feelings. All of this makes food and our food choices as personal as our political and religious beliefs. I often find myself saying to those who find my choices extreme that "it's just food." Well, it is and it isn't. It is in the sense that meals come down to ingredients and if those ingredients, when combined together, taste good—then does it really matter if there are no animal parts in them? And it isn't "just food" when one takes a few moments to reflect on what certain food once was: living, breathing, thinking, feeling beings whose freedom was taken and lives were ended for a filet, a nugget, or a burger on a plate. For me, that choice is difficult to justify when my body can be healthy and thrive with food made from plants rather than of flesh.

I started my plant-based recipe blog, *An Unrefined Vegan*, out of the sheer joy and wonder I felt with my new diet. I wanted to share the incredible food I was discovering—the endless possibilities of flavors, textures, and variety that can be found in good, plant-based food. Like many vegans whom I know, since going plant-based, my food world has expanded far beyond what now seems a very limiting animal-based diet.

It didn't occur to me until I started writing this book that I no longer experience intense cravings unless I've overindulged in heavy, carbohydrate-rich foods—and then that craving is for green, fresh, raw foods. Okay, okay, I admit it. I still absolutely adore peanuts and peanut butter. But I no longer mindlessly dip my spoon straight into the jar, and I only eat natural, unsweetened nut butters. I no longer worry about calories and my weight has stayed the same for years now. Believe me, I'm not perfect. I'm never going to be perfect and that's okay. The key for me is recognizing when I'm starting to head off of the rails into a serious sweet crash and to ask myself why. Am I feeling particularly stressed out? Am I angry about something? Bored? More often than not, the answer to that craving is an emotional need and not a physical one.

And now, just as I no longer reach for a candy bar when I want a treat, instead of taking over-the-counter medications and pain relievers when I'm feeling under the weather or have aches and pains, I bump up my intake of super-healing foods like ginger, green tea, and turmeric.

I'm not a nutritionist or a dietician; I'm just a regular person who slowly learned through self-education and trial and error the importance of giving my body the kind of nourishment it needs and, yes, craves. Your diet may not look like exactly mine, and in fact, it shouldn't. Each one of us has unique emotional, spiritual, and physical connections to food. We all have different health goals and requirements. The purpose of this book and of these tummy-, tooth-, and soul-satisfying recipes is to give you inspiration.

And please, don't buy into the idea that you can't change. That's just nonsense. Look at me: a former sugar-junkie, meat-eating, cheese-loving, cola-addicted couch potato who now exercises every day and dives her fork into a huge, veggie-loaded salad for dinner each night. You can change, too. And you can heal yourself in the process.

Being Vegan, Eating Plant-Based

It took me a while before I understood and appreciated the difference between what it means to be vegan and eating a plant-based diet. I used the terms interchangeably. But there is an important difference.

My transition to a 100% plant-based diet began with the desire to create as much distance between me and doctors, hospitals, and medications as possible. I'd watched family members struggle with major health issues and lost a brother to brain cancer. I was motivated to try almost anything to stay healthy for as long as possible, and eating whole plant food seemed like the best way to do that.

On my journey to better health, however, I picked up a few traveling companions: compassion, perspective, and understanding. Like most humans, I considered myself to be an animal lover—in that disconnected way we, as pet-owners, can have. We adore them for their loyalty and company, for their warmth and furry smell; we're happy when they're happy; we are worried when they are ill or injured, devastated when they leave us forever. And yet, I felt almost nothing for the millions of creatures hauled in from the sea or for animal babies ripped from their mothers or for the innocent beings locked in small cages and prodded, poisoned, and mutilated for the benefit of improved shampoos and eyeliners and medical therapies that rarely correspond to improved treatments for humans. I saw no discrepancy between eating a juicy hamburger coated with cheese and taking every step necessary to assure the health, safety, and long life of my dog.

For me, now, being vegan and eating plant-based are completely intertwined. I went for the health benefits and stayed for the animals.

WHAT'S IN THIS BOOK AND WHAT ISN'T: HOW TO USE THIS BOOK

Chapters

I've done away with traditional cookbook chapters because cravings don't stick to times of day or planned meals. Sure, you'll find breakfast foods, soups, crisp chips, and luscious desserts, but you'll find them in chapters like Salty, Comfort, Crunchy, and Chocolate.

Before you dive into the recipes, keep in mind that this book isn't a "diet." It is not about low-fat eating or deprivation. It is neither a meal plan nor a 30-day program. It simply offers whole food, plant-based recipes designed to healthfully satisfy whatever kind of craving sneaks up on you, no matter what time of day it is.

The Photographs

There is no one but myself to either credit or blame for the photographs that accompany the recipes in this book. My aim was to keep them simple and clean and to highlight the food rather than pretty props (though I do love pretty props) or complicated techniques. I've used my limited skills as photographer and food stylist to try and convey what the typical results will look like when my recipes are prepared. When I acted as hand model, my husband, Kel, stepped behind the camera. Everything you see here was devoured shortly after being photographed.

Sugar, Oil, Gluten & Other Stuff People Worry About

Besides being an animal product-free cookbook, you'll soon notice that there are other familiar ingredients missing—or nearly missing—from these pages. Below is a sampling of some of those along with explanations as to why they are excluded or limited.

White Sugar

As you learned from the introduction to this book, my eating habits have evolved slowly over time as I learned more about what my body needs—craves—to function at its best. One of the first ingredients to fall out of my favor was white sugar. I first eliminated it out of vanity. I wanted to get a flatter stomach. But as I read more about refined sugar, I came to view it—despite its sweet and sparkly allure—as a truly dangerous ingredient.

Have you had those moments during the day when your brain screams, "I need something sweet right now!"?

And after consuming something sugary like a candy bar or soda or a frosted doughnut, did you then feel temporarily contented, as if that inner lion had been tamed? If so, then you might recognize the signs of addiction. Sugar is a highly addicting substance—on par with cocaine. If you don't believe me, go cold turkey on sugar and notice that you suffer from headaches, irritability, fatigue, lightheadedness, and the jitters. Sounds like detox to me.

Sugar also contributes to dangerous belly fat and overall weight gain. Even more frightening, sugar consumption is linked with cancer and rapid cancer growth. It's also linked to the premature aging of cells—from skin cells to brain cells. If you are like me, as you get older, you want to hang onto as many brain cells as possible! Sugar can adversely affect our sleep patterns, create toxicity in our livers, and suppress the hormone that tells our bodies that it's had enough to eat, leading to overeating and weight gain. It also contributes to mineral depletion and fatigue.

The sad thing is that the deck is stacked against us. Big food companies, restaurants, and fast food joints have perfected the science of addiction—trapping our minds and bodies—with unhealthy ingredients like fat, sugar, and salt to assure that we keep coming back for more. When you begin reading ingredient lists you'll see sugar, salt, and fat lurking in the most unlikely places. Even common table salt has sugar in it! In many cases, sugar is listed as the first ingredient because it makes up the largest percentage of the total content.

What about other kinds of sugar? There are many other types of sugars and sweeteners out there: agave nectar, maple syrup, brown rice syrup, stevia, coconut nectar, coconut sugar, date sugar, xylitol, and so on. If a sweetener has been extracted from a whole food and condensed, then my way of thinking is, it's on par with white sugar. This is why I've eliminated most sweeteners from my diet. I've limited sweeteners in my home and in this book to these: fruit, dates, stevia (both in powder and liquid forms), and maple syrup (for more on maple syrup, please read An Explanation of Ingredients Used in This Book on page 10).

My personal sweetener rule of thumb is adopted from Michael Pollan. I only eat sweets on days that begin with S. Unless, of course, my birthday falls on a weekday, in which case—I'm treating myself to something decadent!

Oil

Oil was one of the last items to undergo my scrutiny. Partly because I couldn't imagine being able to cook and bake without it, but also because I loved the taste of olive oil. I'd dip big chunks of ciabatta into it, pour it over salad greens, and add copious amount of it to fresh basil pesto. I believed what I'd read: olive oil was "heart healthy."

This all changed when I learned that oil was just concentrated fat with zero nutritional value. No vitamins, no minerals, no fiber. All it was doing was damaging my arteries, leading me down the road to heart disease.

Okay, Annie. 'Fess up. What about the current wonder substance, coconut oil? You'll see that I use coconut oil sparingly in this cookbook. If you've researched coconut oil even a tad, you've found conflicting information about what it does for the body. It's either a miracle food or worse than guzzling a liter of olive oil. Whatever healthful properties it may have, such as aiding in digestion, preventing candida, facilitating calcium absorption, and on and on, it is best to keep in mind that it is still 100% fat. Go lightly!

Oil vs. Fat

This is not a fat-free cookbook. However, the fats found in these recipes are from whole foods—nuts, seeds, avocados, whole grains—and are accompanied by fiber, vitamins, and minerals. Your body needs healthy fats to function optimally and to absorb and process the vital nutrients found in plants. I recommend treating certain foods in this book as occasional treats rather than daily nosh.

Cooking and Baking without Oil

It took me some time and practice to be able to successfully prepare some foods without a big shot of olive oil. Sauté, roast, and bake without oil?? Is it even possible? It is! Please see Equipment & Techniques on page 28 for a full explanation on how to do it.

Cooking Spray

You'll also notice that on a few occasions I use cooking spray. Nothing makes me crazier than a loaf of bread that sticks to the pan or pancakes that get scrunched on the griddle. My solution is a very light spritz of cooking oil that I then wipe with a paper towel to distribute it evenly inside the pan or muffin tin.

Guest Recipes

You can read more about the Guest Recipes later in this chapter, but briefly—I asked some of my favorite bloggers to contribute recipes to this book. Because they don't all cook the same way that I do, their recipes may contain oils that I do not use, or different kinds of non-sugar sweeteners. I've left their recipes intact with comments about how to make them oil-free or how to swap stevia or maple syrup for other sweeteners.

Gluten

While my body is not gluten-intolerant, I appreciate that many folks out there are opting to exclude it from their diets. First of all, what is gluten? Gluten is a combination of proteins found in certain grains (especially wheat) that produces that familiar chew in baked goods. The reason that yeasted bread dough is kneaded is to develop the gluten which gives the final product that spongy-soft texture. And it's the reason you don't want to stir cookie dough, quick bread, or cake batter too long. Doing so creates a dense product instead of a light, fluffy one. No one wants a spongy brownie that bounces like a basketball when dropped.

So why do people avoid gluten? In people with celiac disease, gluten causes the body to react to the gluten as if it's an enemy invader. This autoimmune response causes damage to the villi in the small intestine—which in turn affects how nutrients are absorbed by the body. Malnutrition is the result. For those with gluten-intolerance, consuming wheat, rye, or barley products (as well as other seemingly unrelated products in which gluten has been added or contamination has occurred) can cause a myriad of symptoms such as "brain fog," severe headaches, dizziness, painful and swollen joints (it's also been linked to rheumatoid arthritis and fibromyalgia), pimpling of the skin on the back on the arms, and depression. Because this book is all about foods that heal the body, I've opted to keep this ingredient to a minimum and to provide gluten-free options.

Protein

Let's (not) talk about protein . . . I don't mention protein much in this book and that's because I don't worry about my protein intake—everyone else who knows I'm vegan does the worrying for me. I kid, but as a plant-based eater, it can get very tiresome being asked about how I get my protein. Here's the short story: I get my protein through plant food like beans, whole grains, soy, greens, and nut butters and milks.

Processed Foods & Convenience Foods

Processed Foods

When I think of processed foods, the image of an orange brick of Velveeta comes to mind, but the term "processed" encompasses many different types of consumables (I hesitate to use the word "food" here) found on grocery shelves. Canned soups and stews, bags of chips, carbonated sodas, packaged doughnuts and cookies, deli meats, frozen meals—all of these are processed foods because they are often made with copious amounts of refined salt, sugar, and fat and chemicals that enhance flavor, make them look more appetizing, and give the products a longer shelf life.

Ask yourself if the item you're holding in your hand came from a farm or a factory, and then take a quick glance at the product's labeling. It will let you know just how bad it is. If the ingredient list is as long as your arm, begins with sugar, and you can't pronounce most of the words—bing!—it's a processed food. These items no longer take up valuable space in my pantry.

Convenience Foods

Some convenience foods are also processed foods, but my own idea of acceptable convenience foods (beyond fresh fruits and vegetables, which are the ultimate in ready-to-eat convenience) are products like canned beans and tomatoes, low-sodium vegetable broths, and frozen fruits and vegetables. You will see that I use canned beans and tomatoes quite a lot in this book; keep in mind you can always substitute dried beans or fresh tomatoes, if you prefer them.

On the Other Hand...

I've been seeing a lot lately about the danger of overly restrictive diets, so I want to add a word of caution and moderation here. There are many who view a vegan diet as restrictive. It is, in the sense that it restricts the consumption and use of animal products. But strictly speaking, that's as far as it goes. In fact, I eat a much more varied diet now that I'm plant-based. A vegan diet does not necessitate the exclusion of gluten, oil or fats, sugar, and/or processed foods. Limiting or eliminating these things is a matter of personal choice, but one must be careful about pedantic dieting. The goal is to be sure that one's body is getting the nutrients necessary to function optimally and to feel healthy. This may take some trial and error. The "diet" that I follow may not be the one that's right for you. Experiment, read, talk to others, and meet with a nutritionist if you feel you aren't getting what you need to feel good. Like a rich, sweet, dark bar of chocolate, life is meant to be savored and enjoyed. If that means having a little oil on your salad or a slice of cake now and again, then do it. Forget the guilt and enjoy each and every bite.

AN EXPLANATION OF INGREDIENTS USED IN THIS BOOK

If you're new to plant-based eating, some of the ingredients I use in the following recipes may be unfamiliar to you. If so, this is a wonderful opportunity to add some delicious, powerhouse staples to your kitchen arsenal! Most of the ingredients are easy to find, especially if you live in a major metropolitan area. I live in a very rural location, so many of these items I have to purchase by mail order. To assist you in finding any products you can't source locally, I've included a list of resources at the end of this book. Below is a list of ingredients with descriptions about how they function in food and what benefits they contribute to our health and well-being.

You'll also notice that many of the recipes are either raw (no ingredients have been cooked above 115 degrees) or high raw (a combination of cooked and raw ingredients). This is because many foods in their raw state provide the highest nutritional (and healing) benefits.

Preparing raw foods requires a shift in thinking. On the one hand, raw can either be the most convenient (and healthiest) "fast food," or it can be the ultimate in slow food. For instance, the Lemon-Spirulina Balls or Laura's Date-Nut Truffles come together in minutes for instant gratification, while the High Raw Blueberry Granola requires nearly 48 hours in the dehydrator.

Agar Agar

Like many other ingredients, agar agar was unknown to me prior to going vegan. A bit pricey, this red (though it is not red in dried form), fiber-rich seaweed is a powerful thickener that I use to make homemade cheez, to thicken cream pie fillings, and to gel jams.

Beans

Beans are my favorite source of plant-based protein and I keep a pantry stocked with as many kinds as I can get my hands on: navy, black, pinto, kidney, great northern, lentil, split pea, black-eyed, and fava—just to name a few. Along with your delicious bowl of beans, you'll get antioxidants and iron, which is key for muscle health and strengthening the immune system. Iron also regulates body temperature, eases insomnia, and supplies oxygen to the blood. Beans are low in fat and have tummy-filling fiber, which helps speed up digestion.

Buckwheat

Although it looks like it, buckwheat is not a grain, but rather is the seed of a flower related to rhubarb. As such, buckwheat is gluten-free. Buckwheat contains manganese, copper, magnesium, and fiber. Buckwheat also contains phosphorus, which is essential for bone and teeth health, and it helps regulate hormones and aids in cell reparation. Consuming buckwheat regularly has been linked with a lowered risk of developing high cholesterol and blood pressure.

Cacao Nibs

I find ways to sneak cacao nibs into just about everything—oatmeal, cookies, pancakes, brownies, sprinkled on top of smoothies—they're satisfyingly crunchy and have a slight bitter-tart flavor. Cacao nibs are broken-up pieces of cacao beans, and while they are not sweet (unless you indulge in the chocolate-covered variety), they do have a wonderful chocolate flavor. Cacao is an excellent source of magnesium—important in nerve and muscle function as well as bone health.

Cacao Powder

Unlike its more-processed counterpart, cocoa powder, cacao powder is considered a raw food because it is milled at temperatures low enough that its nutrients remain. Along with magnesium, antioxidant-rich cacao is a source of iron, calcium, zinc, and copper. Drinking a cup of hot cacao just might help alleviate the effects of stress and anxiety thanks to cacao's potassium content. Potassium also enhances muscle strength and helps the body maintain a healthy balance of water.

Cashews

A seed rather than a nut, cashews are a vegan's best friend when it comes to creating luscious cheeses, sauces, and puddings because of their high starch content. I use them extensively in this cookbook and always have a large stash of them in my freezer. Choose raw cashew pieces (rather than whole) and buy in bulk when possible to save money. Cashews have a slightly sweet taste and are a good source of antioxidants and copper, which helps the body utilize iron, protects against premature aging, and mitigates the symptoms of arthritis. For good measure, cashews also have manganese and magnesium.

Chia Seeds

My first introduction to chia seeds was via the book *Born to Run* by Christopher McDougall, which featured the amazing long-distance running capabilities of the Tarahumara tribe in Mexico. After reading about their energizing and sustaining beverage of choice, chia seeds mixed with water, I got myself a bag of chia seeds and made their beverage a daily ritual. I swear it helped get me through a very emotionally and physically challenging period in my life. Because of their thickening property, chia seeds make a fantastic egg replacer and stand in for gelatin in quick and easy puddings. Their tiny size belies their nutritional punch. Chia seeds are an easy way to get your omega-3 fatty acids as well as zinc, magnesium, and iron. Chia seeds also contain calcium, which as most of us know is important for bone and teeth health, but may also help prevent colon cancer.

Coconut Butter

Not to be confused with coconut oil, coconut butter is simply raw coconut that has been blended until a thick, shiny paste is formed. Coconut butter is commonly used in raw desserts and when creating baked goods with little or no added oil. Unlike the oil, coconut butter is a whole food rather than a refined food.

Coconut Water

This is the slightly milky liquid found inside of a coconut. It's not coconut milk (though it is an ingredient in coconut milk) which is made from the white meat of a coconut. Confused yet? Coconut water has become very popular lately for its beneficial qualities—like amino acids, electrolytes, B vitamins, and more potassium than found in sports drinks (that are loaded with refined sugars). It's not a low calorie food, so consume it mindfully.

Dates/Date Paste

When my supply of Medjool dates gets low—I panic! These date palm fruits are larger than other dates and are deliciously soft and moist, making them an ideal substitute for both oil and sugar in baked goods, smoothies, puddings, sauce, and just about anything that needs sweetening. Dates are loaded with fiber and are a source of potassium, manganese, magnesium, and copper. Date paste is simply dates blended with water to produce a thick, applesauce-like mixture. If you don't have Medjool dates, other varieties will do, but you may need more to achieve the desired sweetness. See my instructions on how to make date paste on page 40.

Ginger Root

Keep a stash of fresh ginger root unwrapped in your produce drawer in the refrigerator so you can add this spicy, flavorful ingredient to your smoothies, soups, curries, and desserts. I like ginger root for its stomach-soothing properties, but it's also beneficial as a pain-killer and anti-inflammatory. It relieves cold and flu symptoms and can help prevent or treat motion sickness, morning sickness, and heartburn.

Goji Berries

These bright red berries taste great on oatmeal, in baked goods, and in trail mixes, and they contain all the essential amino acids. They are high in fiber, protein, and vitamin C. Used in Chinese medicine to treat coughs, fatigue, and headaches, gojis contain zinc, an immune system booster and toxin remover, as well as iron and calcium. Goji berries also contain the antioxidant mineral selenium, which helps protect cells from free radicals.

One caution: if you're taking medications to treat diabetes or high blood pressure, or are on blood thinners, check with your doctor before partaking, as gojis may interfere with the medication's efficacy.

Greens

I'm going to write four blasphemous words: I don't love kale. Sure, its nutritional benefits are much touted. And sure, I eat it regularly and it's featured in this book (just check out my White Bean with Lotsa Kale Soup on page 201), but it's not my favorite green. I much prefer spinach, arugula, romaine, mustard, Swiss chard, and even collards if I can get them when they're young and tender.

Getting a big daily dose of fresh greens may be the single most important thing you do for your body. They are packed with the phytonutrients your body craves—like vitamin C, lutein (for eye health), vitamin E (for healthy skin and protection against sun damage), calcium, potassium, beta-carotene (important for the growth and repair of tissues), and of course lots of fiber and water. To get the maximum benefit from greens, eat them raw—but make sure to chew them very well so that your body can access the nutrients. Or, lightly cook them with a bit of oil, as this acts as a carrier to help get fat-soluble vitamins and minerals like calcium and iron absorbed deep into the body.

Guar Gum

A fine white powder, guar gum is made from guar beans. It's used in gluten-free baking and cooking as a thickener and to improve both texture and shelf-life. It contains fiber, helps the body absorb calcium, and may promote regularity.

Hemp Seeds

Another tiny seed whose size belies its nutritional strengths, hemp seeds are high in protein and are an excellent source of omega-3 fatty acids, which help reduce inflammation. They contain zinc, phosphorus, iron, and magnesium, which helps the body regulate blood pressure and also helps keep our bones strong.

Hibiscus Tea

Not to be confused with the kind of hibiscus with the big red flower, the hibiscus used in tea is made from a bright yellow flower. Regularly sipping tea made from these flowers may help lower blood pressure, control cholesterol, stimulate appetite, and aid with digestive problems. If you already have low blood pressure, ask your doctor about how much is safe for you to consume. If you are pregnant, do not drink hibiscus tea.

Kala Namak or Black Salt

Beloved by vegans for its slightly sulfurous taste and odor that mimic cooked eggs, kala namak is a sea salt that comes from Northern India. I use it here to lend authenticity to my Creamy Scrambled Eggs. Please see Sea Salt (page 16) for more about how I use salt in this book.

Kuzu Powder

A powder made from a root, kuzu is wonderful at thickening and jelling without adding flavor or color. It contains antioxidants and consumption may help relieve stomach cramping.

Liquid Aminos

It's difficult to remember life before liquid aminos! I use this intensely-flavored ingredient in sautéed vegetables, in salad dressings, and as a last minute "finish" to soups and stews. Lucky for us, liquid aminos also come with some great benefits, like containing 16 essential and non-essential amino acids. Because of the soy protein found in liquid aminos, they're associated with a reduced risk of coronary disease and lower cancer risk, especially for breast, colon, and prostate.

Maca

A red, yellow, or black root found in Peru, maca is ground into a fine powder and complements smoothies, baked goods, and plant-based ice creams. Athletes like it for its energy- and performance-enhancing properties. Consumption of this malty-tasting powder helps balance hormone levels and reduces cortisol and adrenaline—those pesky stress-inducing hormones. Partake regularly to relieve depression and lower blood pressure.

Maple Syrup

There's no two ways about it—pure maple syrup is an expensive product. And it's no wonder. To produce one gallon of maple syrup, between 30 and 50 gallons of sap must be collected. The reason is that maple syrup is boiled to reduce the water content—producing that thick, sticky-sweet nectar that we love to pour over our morning pancakes and waffles.

Although maple syrup does contain some manganese, magnesium, riboflavin, zinc, calcium, and potassium, I class it along with other not-so-nice sugars and use it sparingly. I grew up in sugar maple tree country and right down the road from a family who tapped their trees and made their own maple syrup. As a child, I remember being in the sugar house on a frigid late winter day as my neighbor stirred and stirred the steaming syrup. I can still recall the sweet-smoky smell of it and the comforting warmth of the sugar house. It's no wonder that I still adore the rich flavor and beautiful color of maple syrup!

When purchasing maple syrup, go for a high-quality brand or better yet, get it locally if you live in a part of the country that produces this special sweetener.

Mint

Give this plant a toehold in your garden and you might as well forget about growing anything else! But I love it, so my solution is to grow it in pots. That way it's under control and I have fresh mint year-round. Mint leaves are a good source of vitamin A, beneficial for your skin and immune system. I'm drawn to mint for its cool and refreshing taste, but it's also what I crave when my stomach isn't feeling right. I use it here in smoothies, adding the leaves right along with fresh greens for taste and added phytonutrients. Steep fresh mint leaves in hot water for a refreshing and soothing tea. And don't forget to add some chopped fresh mint in stir-fries and Thai curries!

Miso Paste

Rich, salty miso paste is made from fermented soybeans and a fungus called koji or *Aspergillus oryzae*. As unappetizing as this sounds . . . miso is a delicious, versatile ingredient that can be used to impart a salty, cheesy flavor to salad dressings, nut cheeses, stews, and of course as the main flavoring ingredient in miso soup. But miso does more for us than add flavor to foods. Since miso is a cultured food, or live food, its beneficial bacteria help protect us from harmful bacteria and aid our digestive system in absorbing nutrients from other foods. Miso is also good at alkalizing our system and pulling out toxins and heavy metals. Because of its powerful flavor, when adding any type of miso paste to foods, remember that a little goes a long way. Go for unpasteurized varieties since they provide more health benefits and are usually of higher quality.

For those who cannot eat or for those who avoid soy and/or gluten, there are miso pastes made with barley, brown rice, azuki, and other grains and beans. See the Ingredient & Equipment Resources chapter for more information on where to obtain soy- and grain-free miso pastes.

Nutritional Yeast

A lot of vegans will tell you that although they now use copious amounts of nutritional yeast, getting used to it took some practice. I was the same way. My first taste did not leave a good impression, but I stuck with it, learned how and when to use it, and now appreciate both its dense, cheesy, yeasty flavor and its nutritional benefits.

Nutritional yeast is a complete protein, may be a source of the elusive B12 (in fortified varieties), and is low in sodium and fat. To make it, yeast is cultured for several days and then "deactivated" by either freeze-drying or drying (cooking) in a kiln. Unlike live yeast, nutritional yeast is a dark yellow and comes in small or large flakes. For more about nutritional yeast, see the Ingredient & Equipment Resources chapter at the end of this book.

Probiotic Powder

I can't always find vegan yogurt locally so I occasionally add probiotic powder to my daily smoothies. Probiotics help restore beneficial flora in the gut, keeping one's stomach happy and digestion functioning the way that it should. Before purchasing a probiotic powder, make sure that it's vegan.

Sea Salt (unrefined)

This is not a no-salt cookbook, and while I've kept the use of salt to a minimum in these recipes, I understand that for some people, food just doesn't taste right without it. Over the years I've tempered my tastebuds by slowly reducing added salt and by using ingredients that mimic saltiness (such as lemon juice, spices/spice blends, and liquid aminos), so I often don't miss it, but please go ahead and add salt if you like.

I prefer kosher salt for baking bread (not only does it add flavor, it slows down the action of the yeast), but you'll see that in most of the recipes here, I call for sea salt. Although sea salt has about as much sodium as table salt, it does contain trace minerals because it has not been processed. Due to these trace minerals, unrefined sea salt is alkalizing to the body rather than being acidifying, as refined salts are.

Stevia

This plant-based sweetener is my current favorite and helped me wean myself off of refined and other sugars. In its extracted form, stevia is 200–300 times sweeter than white sugar, and it comes in powder and liquid forms. Some experience a slightly bitter aftertaste, but this varies from brand-to-brand and with amount used, so try several brands before giving up.

Spirulina

Look in the dictionary under "green" and you just might see a photo of spirulina powder. This nutrient-dense algae is, like nutritional yeast, a complete protein. It also contains potassium, calcium, copper, iron, selenium, and other nutrients. A great way to get a daily dose of this mighty green powder (also available in cake or flake form) is to put a little in your morning smoothie. Spirulina has a strong taste, so start out with a very small quantity.

Tahini

Slightly less thick than almond or peanut butter, tahini is simply ground sesame seeds, and it's a key ingredient in making velvety hummus. I use it in this book not only for its flavor, but because it makes a great substitute for oil in baked goods, and it's what makes the Sweet Potato Pie and Apple Pie Ice Cream on page 146 so rich and creamy. Tahini contains calcium, protein, and essential fatty acids that keep our skin healthy.

Tapioca Flour

Tapioca flour is a starch derived from the root of the cassava plant. Nutritionally speaking, tapioca flour doesn't provide much benefit (though it is low in fat and sodium), but it is often used in gluten-free flour blends and as a thickener for sauces and gravies.

Teff

Blink and you might miss teff grains. They're a little smaller than poppy seeds, but are tiny powerhouses—providing amino acids, protein, calcium, and iron. If you've eaten at an Ethiopian restaurant, you've probably scooped up those delicious stews with injera—a spongy, fermented flatbread made from ground teff.

I add teff to my morning bowl of oatmeal for its nutty flavor, and I also include it in my Gluten-free All-Purpose

Flour Blend (see recipe on page 42).

Tempeh

A versatile fermented soy product that originated in Indonesia, tempeh is a fine stand-in for meat in many vegan dishes. Although it has a stronger flavor than tofu, it just as readily absorbs marinades and seasonings and has a firm, chewy texture. Because it is a whole food, it has a higher nutritional profile than does tofu—offering more fiber, vitamins, and protein. To ease digestion of tempeh, which is made from partially cooked soybeans, make sure to cook it for 20 minutes. This also removes some of the bitter flavor that can be associated with tempeh.

Tofu

This plant-based champion is made by coagulating soy milk and then pressing it to create thick, dense blocks. Tofu comes in many forms and textures—from fresh to the more processed varieties—as well as what is known as "silken" because of its very delicate, soft texture. Firm tofu's bland flavor profile and sponge-like nature make it the preferred form for marinating and then grilling, baking, or sautéing, while tender silken tofu is wonderful in scrambles, smoothies, pies, and puddings.

Low in calories and high in protein, tofu also contains iron and calcium. If you're feeling adventuresome, make your own tofu at home!

Turmeric Root

I got on the turmeric bandwagon when I began researching my brother's brain cancer and was looking for supplements he could take that might help him as he underwent treatment. Later, I began taking it myself to alleviate a hip injury and to boost my immune system. Like its family member, ginger root, turmeric is a rhizome that can either be eaten fresh or in powdered form. Turmeric is known for its vibrant, deep yellow color and slightly bitter, earthy flavor.

It's the powerful ingredient in turmeric, curcumin, that is the real star of the show here. Curcumin can be taken in extract form to reduce inflammation, which may be a contributing factor in many diseases. Curcumin is also an antioxidant, which means that it fights free radicals—those rogue molecules that can wreak havoc in our bodies. The reason I started my brother on a daily regimen of curcumin was to help curb the replication of cancer cells in his brain. Among other benefits, curcumin has also been linked to improved brain function.

While I prefer to use the fresh root (in smoothies, primarily), I always have the dried powder on hand to add to soups, nut cheeses, curries, and scrambled tofu. You can find fresh turmeric at health food stores or Asian markets.

A FEW WORDS ABOUT SUPPLEMENTS

I wish that all of my nutritional needs were met by eating loads of fresh greens, fruits, vegetables, and whole grains, but try as I might, there are a few holes in my diet. Before I went plant-based I never gave a thought to how much of any nutrient I was absorbing, but it was very clear from everything I read about being vegan that one had to keep tabs on vitamin B12. B12, a bacterium, is not found in plants. The most readily available source of this complex vitamin is through animal products, but animals don't produce B12, they absorb it through soil or water.

So how do vegans get their B12? Since vegans shun animal products, we have to get this vitamin in other ways. One way is by consuming a nutritional yeast (see definition in An Explanation of Ingredients Used in This Book on page 10) that has been fortified; the other way is to take a high-quality vegan supplement. For some, supplements are not properly absorbed, and they may need to get their B12 via injection.

B12 is crucial to the formation of red blood cells, promotes nerve growth, and aids in the production of melatonin, among other things. Fatigue, mental fogginess, sleep issues, getting bruised or bleeding easily, constipation/ diarrhea, and experiencing upset stomach are all symptoms of B12 deficiency. The good news is B12 is stored and used very efficiently by the body, so chances are you're okay with taking the occasional supplement and adding fortified nutritional yeast to your food. The aforementioned symptoms mirror any number of health issues, but if you are concerned, a simple blood test will let you know if you require supplements to boost your levels. It's pretty serious stuff, however. Long-term deficiency may lead to pernicious anemia and to neurological disorders.

The other vitamin everyone—not just vegans—should be mindful of is vitamin D. Called the "sunshine vitamin" because our bodies produce it when our skin is exposed to the sun, many of us are deficient because we don't spend a lot of time outdoors and often when we do we are covered up with clothing. A deficiency in vitamin D is a serious affair. Vitamin D is important for strong bones as it helps our bodies use calcium. If you are experiencing bone and muscle pain, low vitamin D may be your problem. (Persistent muscle soreness and injuries are what led me to getting my D checked—and I was quite low.) Also, a proper level of vitamin D may protect us from certain cancers. Again, a blood test is all it takes to find out if you need to add vitamin D3 pills to your diet. (Supplemental vitamin D is available in two forms, D2 and D3. You want vitamin D3, checking to make sure it is vegan, as some forms of the supplement are made with lanolin.)

I take a daily raw, vegan multi-vitamin each day and additional vitamin D3 (as prescribed by my doctor). This simple regimen works well for me along with the copious amounts of whole, fresh foods that I consume every day. Of course, you should check with your doctor or nurse practitioner before taking any supplements.

A LITTLE HELP FROM MY FRIENDS

The vegan blogging community is a very large but tight-knit group. Over the years I've met and gotten to know and respect bloggers from all around the world. It's one of the really great fringe benefits of social media. As soon as I was sure that this cookbook was going to be a reality, I knew that I wanted to include recipes from my friends—not only because everything is more fun when shared with one's pals, but because they are creative and talented cooks in their own right. The short paragraphs below don't do these dynamic ladies justice, so please be sure to visit their blogs to find out more about them.

Alex requires Italian food at least once a day, be it spaghetti, gnocchi, pesto, or lasagna.

Alex learned how to cook at an early age and had a life centered around the kitchen. This early passion grew into an interest in what best feeds our bodies, so it's no surprise that she went on to study nutrition and public health. Later, she added a degree in exercise science and is now a Registered Dietician, personal trainer, and yoga instructor. Alex's food philosophy can be summed up simply: focus on clean, healthy foods that make you feel like a rock star.

Alex shared Spicy Mushroom Cups on page 238. Find Alex's nourishing "delish" recipes on her site, DelishKnowledge.com

Angela craves crust, be it of the pie or pizza variety.

This chick is one seriously creative cook! Inspired by her joy in eating healthy and healing whole foods and her deep love for animals (especially that handsome feline, Mr. Floyde) of all kinds, she's the very definition of a vegan. Angela sought a plant-based solution to early symptoms of rheumatoid arthritis, and along the way to restoring her health and losing weight, she realized that she could no longer condone the use and abuse of animals to provide us with food and clothing and for medical and product testing.

Angela shared Blueberry "Pit" Pie on page 258 to 259. She blogs about healthy plant-based foods and veganism at Canned-Time.com.

Ashlee craves avocado on toast and can't say no to smoked paprika.

A dedicated and passionate advocate on behalf of all animals, Ashlee Piper is the creator of the vegan food and style site *The Little Foxes*, which aims to show the beauty and elegance in cruelty-free cuisine, clothing, and personal care. Her work has been featured in *AOL*, *Kitchen Daily*, *Refinery29*, *VegNews*, *Vegetarian Times*, *FOX*, *CBS*, *The U*, *Lucky Magazine*, and *Mind Body Green*, to name a few. Ashlee also develops plant-based recipes for the Chicago-based meal delivery service, Home Chef. Red lips and rescue dogs—especially one named Banjo—are her religion.

Ashlee shared Smoky Eggplant Steaks with Balsamic Cashew Cream Sauce & Pine Nuts on page 224. Get your cruelty-free stylishness on with Ashlee at TheLilFoxes.com.

Becky craves creamy and comforting.

Becky is a crafts and food writer from Atlanta, Georgia with a passion for making our planet a healthier, happier, and more compassionate place to live. Her mission is to make vegan food and crafts accessible to everyone! A cozy bowl of soup or a slice of cashew cheese are her go-tos. Becky released her first cookbook—*40 Days of Green Smoothies*—in the fall of 2012. Her new vegan cookbook—*BOWLS!*—came out in the fall of 2014.

Becky shared Gingered Coconut–Sweet Potato Soup on page 295. Eat, repurpose, reuse, and craft along with Becky at GlueandGlitter.com.

Bex craves sweet & sour.

Rebecca (a.k.a.Bex) is a holistic health, lifestyle, and business coach who is passionate about helping women to reignite their sparkle and fall in love with life again. She provides one-on-one coaching, hosts regular wellness events, and is the author of *The Sparkle Experiment*, *Eating for Energy*, *Dessert SuperSmoothies*, and *How to Create a Biz You Love*, as well as being the creator of *The Sparkle Project*.

When she's not dreaming up new ways to help her clients get their glow on, you'll usually find her munching on passionfruit and cuddling random animals.

Bex shared Eggplant Chana Masala on page 117. Reignite your sparkle at VeganSparkles.com.

Brandi craves soft and fluffy cupcakes with lots of frosting.

Brandi is the creator and photographer behind *The Vegan 8*—a website that focuses on simple, delicious, and crave-worthy recipes containing eight ingredients or less. Brandi never fails to impress her readers with her plant-based gluten- and oil-free goodies that utilize healthful ingredients to maximum flavor. This busy wife and mother of an adorable 3-year-old girl makes it her goal to healthfully please the palates of family, friends, and blog followers alike.

Brandi shared Peanut Butter Chocolate Chip Espresso Brownies on page 261. Grab your mixing bowl and big spoon and visit Brandi at TheVegan8.com.

Dianne craves anything in the food group Chocolate.

Dianne is a Jane-of-all-trades. She is a vegan health and lifestyle coach, social media consultant, artist, writer, blogger, crafter, and self-confessed crazy cat lady. She lives in northern New Jersey, where she teaches cooking classes, runs a busy vegan meet-up group, and works to promote veganism in the local community.

Dianne shared Green & White Pizza on page 74. Keep up with Dianne at her website, DiannesVeganKitchen.com.

Gabby is an equal opportunity craver who reaches for chocolate, sushi, tempeh, coffee, or lemon water.

Gabby Ouimet is food obsessed. Cooking and eating are her absolute favorite activities, and as a holistic nutritionist she gets to talk about food all day long! She is also working towards her Masters of Public Health, hoping to bring holistic lifestyle principles into wider practice. In her spare time, she is a blogger, crafter, knitter, reader, amateur coffee and wine enthusiast, and adventurer, whether it be at home or in a faraway land.

Gabby shared Oatmeal Creme Brûlée on page 177. Obsess over food with Gabby at her website, VeggieNook.com.

Kathy craves masala dosas when she's not craving beets or beans.

No one does comfort food like Kathy Hester. The author of *The Vegan Slow Cooker*, *The Great Vegan Bean Book*, *Vegan Slow Cooking for Two*, and *OATrageous Oatmeals*, Kathy creates simple, delicious, and nutritious plant-based eats from her home in North Carolina—inspired by one picky eater and a couple of cats and dogs. As if all that cooking doesn't keep her busy enough, Kathy is a freelance writer, a cookbook promoter, and an inspiration to vegan food bloggers everywhere.

Kathy shared Whole Wheat Veggie Quinoa Drop Biscuits on pages 78 and 79. Set your slow cooker on low and visit Kathy at HealthySlowCooking.com.

Kristy craves peanut butter.

Kristy Turner is the writer, recipe developer, and food stylist behind the blog *Keepin' It Kind* and author of the book, *But I Could Never Go Vegan!*. Former fromagier and mutterer of the words, "I could never be vegan," Kristy now loves her compassionate lifestyle and works with her photographer husband, Chris, to make veganism accessible, fun, and delicious for everyone.

Kristy shared Maple-Glazed Cinnamon Roasted Chickpeas on page 171. Go vegan with Kristy at KeepinItKind.com.

Laura craves maple syrup, potatoes, and lemon—but not together.

Laura, a.k.a. The Jazzy Vegetarian, is a gracious and dedicated ambassador for both the plant-based eating and vegan lifestyles, sharing her delicious, simple, and healthful recipes via her popular radio and television shows and two cookbooks—*Jazzy Vegetarian: Lively Vegan Cuisine That's Easy* and *Delicious and Jazzy Vegetarian Classics: Vegan Twists on American Family Favorites*. Laura is also an award-winning jazz singer and actor who has been featured in newspapers and magazines such as *The New York Times*, *Vegetarian Times*, *Variety*, and *VegNews*, among others, as well as on many news and entertainment television shows.

Laura shared Date-Nut Truffles on page 265. Find Laura's recipes at JazzyVegetarian.com and get ready to sing at LauraTheodore.com.

Poppy craves carbs and chocolate, especially when they take the form of chocolate cake.

Poppy is currently studying for a degree in Animal Management, and she shares her heart and time caring for and helping to rehabilitate animals at the Wildlife Hospital so that they can be released back into their natural habitats. As passionate about food as she is about animal welfare, Poppy is on a mission to visit as many vegetarian restaurants in the United Kingdom as possible. Throw in a few castles and gardens and she is one happy vegan. Poppy shares her home with twelve bunnies, two cats, and three degus.

Poppy shared Mexican Chocolate Cake on page 107. Hop on (I couldn't resist!) over to Poppy's blog at BunnyKitchen.com.

Richa craves cayenne and hot chilies.

Sidelined from her software development job in 2006 while she recovered from surgery to remove a meningioma (a type of brain tumor), Richa decided it was time to pursue other career options. Lucky for us, Richa turned to cooking, baking, and food photography, and in 2009, her blog *Vegan Richa* was born. On *Vegan Richa*, you'll find main dishes, soups, stews, breads, desserts, and everything in between that are heavily influenced and inspired by her Indian heritage. Richa focuses on gluten-free, low-sugar, low-oil recipes that are as beautiful as they are delicious.

A dedicated animal advocate, Richa acts as foster parent for the Seattle Humane Society and Dog Rescue. She is also the proud "parent" of an adorable fluffball named Chewie.

Richa shared Red Lentil Quinoa Cauliflower Stew on page 252. Keep your eye out for Richa's first cookbook and follow her along with hundreds of thousands of loyal fans at VeganRicha.com.

Sarah is a year-round craver of pumpkin.

A culinary school graduate with a degree in photography, Sarah's skills in the kitchen and her passion for good food were being wasted as a food service employee. Pregnancy and the movie *Earthlings* completely changed Sarah's views about animals, and in 2006 she went vegan. She is a stay-at-home mom to two beautiful kids.

Sarah shared Raw Almond & Goji Berry Chocolate Bark on page 111. Sarah shares her love of creating compassionate cuisine at MyDarlingVegan.com.

Somer craves comfort foods.

Diagnosed with ulcerative colitis in 2006, Somer struggled with severe and debilitating gastrointestinal problems and the attendant side effects of prescription medications, such as extreme weight gain and acne. With a lot of hard work and dedication, Somer was able lose the excess weight and to bring her symptoms under control, but the dependence on harsh drugs and many frustrating setbacks were taking their toll. As it has for so many, the movie *Forks Over Knives* changed Somer's life forever and she and her family made the transition to a plant-based, whole foods diet. She credits her animal-free diet with allowing her to ditch the prescription medications, for losing the extra pounds, and for restoring her physical and emotional health. Somer's first cookbook, *The Abundance Diet: The 28-Day Plan to Reinvent Your Health and Lose Weight Through the Power of Whole Foods*, comes out in the spring of 2015.

Somer shared Tempeh Tacos on page 213. Get inspired by Somer's story as well as her homey, comforting recipes at VedgedOut.com.

Teresa craves toast, hot chocolate, and coffee.

A combination of health reasons, environmental concerns, spiritual growth, and a compassion for animals inspired Teresa to go vegan. Focusing on macrobiotic and healing foods, Teresa has a degree in Community Health and is a Reiki Master and a trained macrobiotic chef.

Teresa shared Black Soybeans with Chestnuts & Shiitake Mushrooms on page 131. When she's not mountain biking or walking barefoot in the rain, Teresa creates simple, energy-giving, healing recipes at SweetVeg.org and LittleVeg.com.

Tracey craves salt. Then sweets. Then salt.

A life-changing trip to Rishikesh, India, guided Tracey on the path to inner peace, balance, and harmony through yoga and meditation. While there, she earned her Yoga Alliance teacher certification and now helps others find their inner peace via yoga classes in Mobile, Alabama. A lifelong animal lover and advocate, Tracey turned to veganism for ethical reasons, but also for her health, and for the health of the planet. It only made sense, then, that Tracey went on to earn her certification by the American Fitness Professionals & Associates as a Nutrition and Wellness Consultant.

Tracey regularly appears on local television, where she shares simple and approachable plant-based recipes to viewers. She also contributes to the online yoga and wellness publication *Elephant Journal*. If you are lucky enough to live in Mobile, you can order Tracey's delicious and wholesome vegan meals for home delivery via her company, The Pure Vegan.

Tracey shared Roasted Veggie Phyllo Pillows on pages 308 and 309. Practice, meditate, and eat with Tracey at ShantiWarrior.com.

BUILDING
BLOCK
RECIPES

EQUIPMENT & TECHNIQUES

Before diving into the food, I thought it might be helpful to describe some of the equipment I use in my kitchen—and therefore in this book. There are a few big ticket items, but if you have a blender and an oven, you should be good to go. I follow this with a short section on technique—well, mostly how to cut tofu into slabs, slices, and cubes—with pictures! After that, we finally get into some recipes—what I call Building Block Recipes—that will give you a foundation on which to build your own recipes and meals. I also use many of these building blocks to complement the recipes in this book.

Equipment

Dehydrator

Could someone live their life without ever owning a dehydrator? After all, they're bulky, loud, and expensive, and you've probably gotten this far without needing one. Believe me, I get it. Purchasing a dehydrator was very low on my list until I made a commitment to adding more raw foods to my diet (and to forgoing store-bought chips and crackers).

Dehydrators open up a whole range of culinary possibilities, from making dried fruit without sugars or preservatives and healthy, oil- and additive-free crackers and breads to fruit leathers and delicious, raw, gluten-free cookies. They also come in a range of sizes, shapes, and prices—so if you don't already own one, you may want to do a little research. It will become an integral part of your cooking. If you take the dehydrator plunge, be sure to invest in Teflexx (flexible, non-stick) sheets.

Food Processor

In some instances, a food processor can stand in for a blender, and in some cases, nothing but a food processor will do. I use mine when making the dough for raw breads, crackers, and cookies and to finely chop veggies. It doesn't do so well with very liquid ingredients, but it's a champ for everything else.

High-speed Blender

This is another luxury kitchen item that has become indispensable in my kitchen. I used to go through at least one $19.99 bargain blender per year. They just couldn't handle what I wanted them to do. So I swallowed hard and purchased a Vitamix, and I don't regret the expenditure for a second. I use my blender 3 to 4 times a day.

You read that right: 3 to 4 times per day. It's just the thing for making super-creamy salad dressings, puddings, sauces, nut and seed milks, and thick greens- and fruit-packed smoothies.

Juicer

Prior to my sister giving me her old juicer, I'd never even considering adding this item to my kitchen arsenal. I am, however, very glad that I have it. Juicing every day is a bit too time-consuming for me—and I prefer smoothies because of the additional fiber—but a couple of times a week, a refreshing juice made with a variety of fruits, vegetables, and roots really perks me up and makes my tastebuds sing.

Nut Milk Bag

This goes hand-in-hand with a high-speed blender and making nut or seed milks at home. Often this item will come with the purchase of a high-speed blender, but you can easily get one for $10.00 or less at kitchen stores or online.

Silicon Baking Sheet/Parchment Paper

These are essential in oil-free baking and roasting. Place a sheet on your baking pan and your cookies, vegetable burgers, and rolls will lift off easily without added oil. P.S. Do not use either silicon mats or parchment paper when broiling!

Tofu Press

At first blush, this may seem like an extravagant item to have in one's cupboard. I thought so until I tried one. Consider me a convert. Tofu takes on a totally different personality when it spends a few hours in a press. You wouldn't believe how much liquid comes out! Removing the liquid makes room for delicious marinades to get deep into that bland block of tofu.

Techniques

How to Water or Broth Sauté

You'll see that in many recipes I instruct to "water sauté" or "broth sauté." This means that in place of oil, use water, vegetable broth, or even liquid aminos or tamari to sauté. Once you get the hang of it, cooking without oil is a cinch. Here's how I do it:

Heat a skillet or pan over medium heat and add a couple of tablespoons or so of water, vegetable broth, or liquid aminos (see An Explanation of Ingredients Used in This Book for more on this product). Add veggies or tofu and stir occasionally, letting the liquid almost cook off. Add more liquid and continue to cook until veggies are tender—or to the consistency you desire.

The same technique works for "roasting" vegetables or tofu in the oven. See Lemon-Garlic Baked Tofu on page 285 for a full description, but simply, you want to have liquid in the pan with whatever you are roasting, letting it cook off before adding more. You'll soon find that you don't miss the oil.

Baking is a bit different and often I will use just a little bit of coconut oil for texture and flavor—but it is possible to make cakes and cookies completely without oil. Just don't expect them to bake or taste exactly like their oil- and shortening-rich counterparts. For full descriptions about baking without oil (or with limited oil), please see individual recipes, such as Orange Pecan Mini Banana Breads on page 80 or Coconut-Lime Mini Doughnuts on pages 106 and 107.

Cutting Tofu

There are many ways to cut tofu (firm, not silken)—and they're all very difficult to describe! So I've put together some photos that walk you through the various steps of cutting tofu into large slabs (good for sandwiches), planks (ideal for stuffing into pitas or tortillas), cubes (for stir-fries or soups), and thin, wide strips (great for making "bacon"). Use these examples for the Tofu Gyros (page 234) and Lemon-Garlic Baked Tofu (page 285)—or for any time you are puzzling over the blank canvas that is a block of tofu.

Because tofu is like a thirsty sponge, it absorbs a lot of water when packaged. If you don't remove the water, it dilutes any sauces or seasonings that are added to the tofu—so I always take the extra step of pressing the tofu prior to marinating or seasoning. In fact, I always have a block of tofu pressing in the refrigerator so I'm ready to go when the mood strikes. If you don't have a handy tofu press, line a plate with paper towels, place the tofu on top of the paper towels and place more towels on top of the tofu. Put another plate on top of the towels and add a couple of heavy cans (or books) on top of the plate. Move the cans around to get an even pressing. Let the tofu sit for a few hours, then remove the cans, plate, and paper towels, drain, and proceed with the recipe.

Slabs

Thick Planks

Follow steps 1 through 4 and then:

Cubes

Follow steps 1 through 6 and then:

Slices

When I cut tofu into thin slices, I often freeze them so that they acquire a firmer, chewier texture. To freeze, cut as shown below, line a small baking sheet with paper towels and then with parchment (which won't stick to the tofu), and lay out the strips in one layer. Cover with additional parchment and paper towels and place in the freezer overnight. The tofu will turn yellow, but will return to its former white color once thawed. Dab to remove extra moisture and remove

from the pan, and the tofu is ready to be marinated with your favorite sauces/seasonings and cooked.

Soaking Nuts and Seeds

This cookbook makes heavy use of nuts and seeds and you'll notice that I often instruct to soak them for a few hours (and sometimes overnight) before use. This does two things. First, it softens them so that they process better, resulting in a wonderfully smooth texture, not to mention less wear and tear on your blender or food processor. The second reason is more important. Nuts and seeds are protected by something called enzyme inhibitors. This protection lasts until the nut or seed has the ideal conditions in which to sprout and grow, i.e., moisture. When we consume raw nuts and seeds that have not been soaked, we are missing out on a lot of their nutritional benefits and we may be hindering the digestive process as well. When nuts and seeds are soaked in water, these inhibitors break down, making the vital nutrients more bioavailable to our bodies.

Soaking is also the first step in sprouting—which takes the process one step further. See pages 43 through 45 for instructions on how to sprout grains, nuts, and seeds.

ALMOND MEAL OR ALMOND-COCONUT MEAL

makes about 2 cups

The dehydrator is a convenient way to evenly and thoroughly dry nut meals. A quick zap in the food processor after drying assures a fine meal with no clumps. Store the meal in an air-tight container in the freezer. You can also dry whole soaked nuts and seeds in the dehydrator.

1 batch pulp from almond milk (see recipe on page 35) or almond-coconut milk (see recipe on page 153)

▸ After preparing almond milk, scrape the almond (or almond-coconut) meal out of the nut bag onto one or two non-stick dehydrator sheets, depending on the size of your dehydrator. Dehydrate the meal for 2 to 3 hours at 115 degrees, or until it is dry and crumbly.

▸ Place the meal in the bowl of a food processor and pulse until the meal is fine. Store in an air-tight container in the refrigerator or freezer.

Suggestions

▸ Use almond or almond-coconut meal to make "Parmesan" Cheez (see recipe on page 54).

▸ Use almond or almond-coconut meal in baked goods.

Gluten-free ▲ Oil-free ▲ Raw ▲ Easy

Total time: **3 hours**

ALMOND MILK

makes 4 cups

Making nut milks at home is very easy and the result is pure, silky, additive-free bliss. Add your favorite flavored extract and/or sweetener to create customized, craveable milk.

2 cups raw almonds, soaked 8 to 12 hours, rinsed and drained
3 1/2 to 4 cups filtered water

▶ Place almonds and water in a high-speed blender and process for about 1 minute. Check the consistency. Add more water if you prefer thinner milk.
▶ Place a nut bag or fine-mesh colander over a large bowl or large measuring cup. Pour the almond mixture into the bag/colander. If using a nut bag, squeeze it to extract as much milk out of it as you can.
▶ Store milk in the refrigerator for up to 5 days. Reserve the almond pulp, dehydrate, and use in baked goods, crackers, or in the "Parmesan" Cheez recipe on page 54.

Suggestions

▶ Use your favorite nut instead of almonds.

Gluten-free ▲ Oil-free ▲ Raw ▲ Easy
Total time: 12 hours (soaking) and 10 minutes

Building Block Recipes

CASHEW COCONUT CREAM CHEEZ

makes about 1 cup

The first time I made this, I wasn't thinking about creating a cream cheese substitute, but that's what happened. I surprised myself by coming up with a smooth, slightly tangy, salty substitute for the real thing.

1 cup raw cashews, soaked 8 to 12 hours, rinsed and drained

1/4 cup Coconut Butter (see page 37 for recipe) or 1/4 cup unsweetened coconut flakes, soaked for 15 minutes and drained

1 Tbsp. white miso paste

1/4 cup fresh lemon juice

1/4 tsp. pure maple syrup, or to taste

Pinch sea salt

▶ Add all of the ingredients to a high-speed blender or food processor and process until very smooth. You'll need to scrape down the sides of the bowl a few times. It will take several minutes to get a truly creamy cheez.

▶ Line a mini-loaf pan or other small/shallow dish with several layers of cheesecloth. Scrape the cheez into the prepared dish and pat down and smooth the top. Fold over the edges of the cheesecloth and put the cheez in the refrigerator. Let cheez rest in the refrigerator for 24 hours before serving.

Suggestions

▶ If you use the Coconut Butter rather than the coconut flakes, you may need to add just a touch of water when processing.

▶ If you don't have miso, try using one tablespoon of nutritional yeast instead.

▶ The brand of miso used will affect the sweetness of this cheez, so you may wish to taste the mixture prior to adding the maple syrup.

Gluten-free ▲ Oil-free ▲ High Raw ▲ Easy

Prep time: **12 hours (including soaking time)**

Cook time: **10 minutes (plus 24 hours rest)**

COCONUT BUTTER

makes about 1 1/3 cups

Expensive to buy, easy to make at home, coconut butter is a luscious ingredient in raw desserts and baked goods. I have to control myself not to eat this with a spoon.

4 cups raw, unsweetened coconut chips

▷ Put the coconut chips in the bowl of a food processor. Process for 10 to 15 minutes, scraping the sides of the bowl down occasionally, until you have a thick, slightly shiny paste.

▷ Store coconut butter indefinitely in an air-tight container in the refrigerator. Coconut butter hardens when chilled, so let it come to room temperature before using, or warm gently and carefully in the microwave.

Gluten-free ▲ Oil-free ▲ Raw ▲ Easy
Total time: **15 minutes**

CAYONNAISE

makes 1 cup

Cashews and non-dairy yogurt combine to make—cayonnaise! Thanks to the yogurt, this mayo is a bit more like salad dressing-style mayo, but the flavors blend and mellow over time, resulting in a very rich sandwich spread.

3/4 cup plain non-dairy yogurt
1/4 cup raw cashew pieces, soaked for a
    few hours, rinsed and drained
2 tsp. fresh lemon juice
1 tsp. white miso paste

1/2 tsp. nutritional yeast
1 small clove garlic
1/4 tsp. kala namak (black salt) or a pinch
    of sea salt

▶ Put all ingredients in a high-speed or regular blender and process until silky smooth, scraping down the sides of the blender as necessary.
▶ Pour cayonnaise into a glass container and store in the refrigerator for up to 10 days.

Suggestions

▶ Unsweetened plain yogurt is as elusive as Bigfoot, but if you can find it, use it instead for a less-sweet CaYo.
▶ This mayonnaise gets thicker and even tastier after a few days in the refrigerator.
▶ The black salt gives this a slightly "eggy" scent and flavor.
▶ Use this recipe as a base for the Chipotle-Lemon Aioli Dip & Dunk Sauce (see recipe on pages 216 and 217).

Gluten-free ▲ Oil-free ▲ Easy
Total time: **5 minutes**

DATE PASTE

makes 2 cups

It doesn't get much easier than this—and this simple, rich paste is the answer to adding healthy sweetness to just about anything that needs it.

2 cups Medjool dates, pitted and roughly
      chopped
1 1/2 cups cool or room temperature
      water

▶ Soak the dates in the water for 2 to 4 hours. Pour the mixture into a high-speed blender or food processor and process until very smooth. Add more water if the consistency is too thick.

▶ Put the date paste in a sealed container and store in the refrigerator for 7 to 10 days.

Suggestions

▶ If you don't have a high-speed blender, the soaking time may need to be longer.

Gluten-free ▲ Oil-free ▲ Raw ▲ Easy
Total time: **2 hours + 5 minutes (including soaking time)**

GLUTEN-FREE ALL-PURPOSE FLOUR BLEND

makes 9 1/2 cups

Although I'm much more comfortable working with wheat flours, I've added more gluten-free baked goods to my repertoire, so I decided it was time to make my own blend to keep costs down and to adapt it to my tastes. Feel free to use your own favorite blend or brand, but results in taste and texture will vary.

6 cups brown rice flour
2 cups potato starch
1 cup tapioca starch
1/2 cup teff flour

▶ Combine all ingredients in a large bowl and mix thoroughly. Transfer to an air-tight container and store in the refrigerator or freezer.

Gluten-free ▲ Oil-free ▲ Easy
Total time: **10 minutes**

BROCCOLI SEED SPROUTS

Before I knew better, I'd pick off the mung bean sprouts that were sprinkled on top of fried rice and pad thai at Asian restaurants. To me, they were just decoration that got in the way of the real food underneath. Little did I know that I was discarding the most nutritious part of the meal! Nuts, seeds, grains, and beans are packed with everything that a tiny plant will need to get a good start in life: chlorophyll, protein, and concentrated nutrition and energy. In plants, chlorophyll transforms sunlight and CO_2 into sugar and oxygen. When we ingest chlorophyll, it helps our blood absorb oxygen (possibly due to high amounts of iron and manganese), which in turn may assist in the function, growth, and repair of our cells. Chlorophyll also may help protect our bodies from the effects of radiation and help wounds heal faster.

You don't need a vast amount of acreage or even a whole bunch of clay pots—or time—to grow your own nutrient-dense food. If you've got some mason jars, water, seeds, nuts, grains, and/or beans, you can grow your own sprouts in just a few day's time. Then you are ready to add these adorable superfoods to your salad, sandwiches, smoothies, raw breads, and stir-fries. While some grains (such as wheatgrass) and seeds are more successfully sprouted in soil, I'm going to focus on those that can be easily sprouted in water. I've chosen broccoli seeds as my example—but feel free to try your hand at radish, alfalfa, chia, lentils, rice—the list goes on! Most of these require a soaking time of between 5 hours to 12 hours and between 1 to 4 days to reach harvest. In addition to the nutritional benefits of eating sprouts, you have the comfort of knowing that your sprouts are very fresh and as long as you are working with clean hands, a clean jar, and filtered water—are free of scary bacterial critters.

soak

1 (1-quart) clean mason jar with ring
1 Tbsp. broccoli seeds
4 Tbsp. filtered water
Small piece cheesecloth

rinse/drain

▶ Place the seeds in the mason jar and add the filtered water. Cover the jar opening with the cheesecloth, secure with the ring, and let the jar sit for 7 to 8 hours. Drain the water and rinse the seeds a few times. Drain thoroughly and set the jar at a 45-degree angle (this allows for better air circulation) in a dark place.

▶ Twice a day, rinse and drain the sprouts and set at a 45-degree angle in a dark spot. When the little sprouts are 2 to 3 times as long as the original seed/nut/grain, place the jar in a sunny spot for 15 to 20 minutes to allow them to green up a bit.

▶ Your sprouts are now ready to eat! You'll want to consume them fairly quickly to enjoy their maximum nutritional benefits, but you can store the sprouts in the refrigerator for a few days. Just make sure that the sprouts remain moist, but not wet.

Suggestions

▶ You can also get a jar with a ventilated lid made just for sprouting. If you are going to be sprouting a large variety or amount of seeds or grains at one time, you may wish to invest in stacked, ventilated trays.

harvest

HIGH RAW CORN TORTILLAS

makes 10 to 12

The ingredient list is a little long, but the dehydrator does most of the work. These smell incredible as they're baking.

1 cup flaxseed meal
1 Tbsp. cumin
1/2 Tbsp. chili powder
1/2 tsp. turmeric
1/2 tsp. garlic powder
1/2 tsp. ground black pepper
Pinch cayenne
Zest of 1 lime
2 1/2 cups frozen corn, thawed and
drained
1 large carrot, peeled and cut into chunks
1/2 cup red onion, chopped
1/2 cup fresh cilantro
3/4 cup vegan Mexican lager or lager
1 Tbsp. dried onion flakes
Juice of 1 lime
Pinch sea salt

▶ In a large bowl, whisk together the flaxseed meal, cumin, chili powder, turmeric, garlic powder, black pepper, cayenne, and lime zest. Set aside.
▶ Place the remaining ingredients in the bowl of a food processor and pulse until the ingredients are very finely chopped, but you should still see small bits of carrot, cilantro, onion, and corn. Scrape this mixture into the flaxseed meal mixture and stir thoroughly. You don't want any dry bits.
▶ Divide the mixture into 12 equal portions using a ¼ cup measurer. Working with one portion at a time, place on a non-stick dehydrator sheet and shape into a circle that is about 5 inches in diameter (it should be about ¼ inch thick). Proceed with the remaining portions—four tortillas per dehydrator tray.
▶ Set the dehydrator to 145 degrees and dehydrate the tortillas for 30 minutes. Turn down the heat to 115 degrees and continue to dry the tortillas until very firm and crispy, 12 to 20 hours.

Suggestions
▶ Add a tablespoon of nutritional yeast for a cheesy tortilla flavor.
▶ After 2 to 3 hours in the dehydrator, carefully flip the tortillas by placing a mesh dehydrator sheet fitted into another tray on top of the dough. Flip and gently remove the non-stick sheet. Place the tray back in the dehydrator. This will speed up the drying time.
▶ If you prefer a softer, more pliable tortilla, check texture after about 5 hours.

Gluten-free ▲ Oil-free ▲ Raw Option ▲ Easy

Total time: **12+ hours**

"SAUSAGE" PATTIES

makes 8

Although I enjoy seitan-based sausages—both the kind I make at home and those that are commercially available—I wanted to create something that was wheat-free so that everyone could enjoy it. The flavors in these patties are pure Italian sausage, which you will smell as they are baking.

1 cup buckwheat groats
2 cups water
1 cup vegan dry red wine
1 garlic clove, chopped
1 tsp. dried rosemary
4 whole cloves
2 Tbsp. tahini
1 tsp. ground black pepper

1 tsp. poultry seasoning
1/2 tsp. fennel seeds
1/2 tsp. sea salt, optional
Dash red pepper flakes
2 garlic cloves, finely minced or microplaned
2 Tbsp. arrowroot powder
1/2 cup gluten-free rolled oats

Put the buckwheat groats in a small saucepan and add 2 cups of water. Cook for about 12 minutes, or until most of the water has cooked off and the groats are tender. Let cool slightly and then remove ¾ cup of the groats and pulse in a food processor until fairly smooth. Return to the pan with the whole groats, stir and set aside.

In another small saucepan, bring the wine, garlic clove, rosemary, and whole cloves to a boil. Reduce the heat to medium-low and simmer the wine for about 15 minutes. Remove from the heat and strain, discarding the solids. Stir the wine mixture and the tahini in with the buckwheat groats. Set aside.

In a large bowl, whisk together the remaining ingredients. Add the buckwheat groats mixture and stir until the ingredients are thoroughly combined and the mixture is the consistency of a thick dough. Cover the bowl and refrigerate the mixture for about an hour.

Preheat the oven to 425 degrees. Line a large baking sheet with a silicone baking mat or parchment paper. Using a ⅓ cup measure, scoop up the buckwheat mixture, pack it down, and then gently tap the cup on the palm of your hand to release the mixture. Place patty on the prepared baking sheet and pat down the mixture, using wet fingers, to about a ½-inch thick disk. Continue with the remaining mixture.

Bake the "sausage" patties for 15 minutes, then gently flip them and continue to bake an additional 10 to 15 minutes. The outside will be dark and crispy. Serve immediately, or let patties cool and store them in an airtight container in the refrigerator for up to 5 days.

Suggestions

These patties are crispy on the outside and tender on the inside, but the outside will soften a bit after being stored in the refrigerator.

Gluten-free ▲ Oil-free ▲ Easy

Prep time: **1 hour 15 minutes** *Cook time:* **25–30 minutes**

MOM'S MARINARA SAUCE

makes about 5 cups

Although my mom makes a killer slow-cooked pasta sauce, I thought her quick weeknight marinara sauce was almost as good. My favorite way to eat it was with pillowy gnocchi, but this works great as a pizza or calzone sauce as well.

1/4 cup water for sautéing
1 medium onion, finely chopped
1 clove garlic, minced
1/4 cup dry red wine, optional
1 tsp. dried oregano
1 tsp. dried basil

1 tsp. dried onion flakes
Pinch ground black pepper
1 (28-ounce) can crushed tomatoes
1 (15-ounce) can petite-diced tomatoes
1 Tbsp. Date Paste (see recipe on page 40)

▶ In a large skillet, heat the water over medium-high heat and sauté the onion for 5 to 8 minutes, or until translucent. Add the garlic and cook an additional 1 to 2 minutes. Stir in the red wine, if using, and cook until most of the wine has cooked off. Stir in the oregano, basil, onion flakes, and black pepper and cook an additional 1 to 2 minutes.

▶ Add the crushed tomatoes, diced tomatoes, and the date paste and stir well to combine. Turn the heat to low and simmer the sauce for 30 minutes, stirring occasionally. If you have a mesh splash guard, this is the time to use it, as the sauce will bubble and spurt like a hot spring at Yellowstone. Taste and adjust the seasonings.

Suggestions
▶ If you like a smoother sauce, blend some or all of the marinara.

Gluten-free ▲ Oil-free ▲ Easy
Total time: **45 minutes**

Building Block Recipes

MULTIGRAIN PIZZA DOUGH

makes two pizzas

The inspiration for this dough comes from Peter Reinhart's beautiful bread book, The Bread Baker's Apprentice, *and specifically his recipe for a loaf he calls "Multigrain Extraordinaire." It's one of the most flavorful loaves of bread I've ever eaten and it calls for a pre-soak of various grains. Soaking the grains activates enzymes, makes them more digestible, and brings out their natural sugars.*

1 Tbsp. millet (uncooked)	3 1/2 cups whole wheat flour
1 Tbsp. quinoa (uncooked)	1/4 cup vital wheat gluten
2 Tbsp. rolled oats (uncooked)	3 Tbsp. cooked brown rice
4 Tbsp. water	1 tsp. sea salt
1 1/3 cup non-dairy milk, gently heated	1 tsp. dried oregano
1 Tbsp. active dry yeast	1 tsp. dried thyme
1 Tbsp. pure maple syrup	1/4 tsp. ground black pepper
1 Tbsp. coconut oil, melted	

▶ In a small bowl, combine the millet, quinoa, and rolled oats with the 4 tablespoons of water. Cover with plastic wrap and let sit overnight.

▶ The next day, in the bowl of a stand-mixer, combine the warm non-dairy milk, yeast, maple syrup, and coconut oil. Let sit until the yeast begins to bubble. Add the remaining ingredients and, using the paddle attachment, stir until the ingredients are mixed thoroughly and the dough comes together. Switch to the hook attachment and knead the dough for 6 to 8 minutes. The dough should be slightly sticky to the touch, but if it feels too sticky, add a little bit more flour and mix in.

▶ Lightly spray a large bowl with cooking oil and place the dough in the bowl, cover, and let sit at room temperature for an hour or until the dough has doubled in size.

▶ Once the dough has doubled, you can either divide the dough in two, wrap, and freeze it all—or freeze one portion and make one pizza using the following method.

▶ Preheat the oven to 500 degrees. If you're going to use a baking stone, place the stone in a cold oven and then turn on the heat. If you're using a baking pan, line it with parchment paper. Punch down the dough and lightly flour your work surface. Using a rolling pin, roll the dough to a 12 or 15 inch circle. Place the dough on the prepared pan—or if you're using a baking stone, line the bottom of a baking pan with parchment and place the dough on top of that. This way you can easily slide the dough and the parchment directly onto the baking stone. Using a fork, make small holes all over the dough. Let the dough rise for about 15 minutes.

▶ Place the dough in the oven and bake for 5 minutes. Carefully remove the crust and add your favorite sauce and toppings or make Dianne's Green and White Pizza on page 74. Bake the pizza for an additional 5 to 10 minutes. The sides and bottom of the pizza should be deeply browned. Slice pizza into 6 pieces and serve.

Prep time: **1 hour 30 minutes, plus soaking time**
Bake time: **10–15 minutes**

CASHEW BUTTER

makes about 1 cup

The truth is, I rarely make my own nut butters. This isn't because it's difficult to do, but rather because it's a whole heck of a lot easier for me to take advantage of those industrial-sized nut grinders at health food stores, or to buy a jar of natural, no-sugar nut butters. However, it's fun to give it a try, and the taste really is wonderfully fresh.

Making nut or seed butters is similar to making Coconut Butter (see recipe on page 37). Throw the nuts in the food processor or high-speed blender and several minutes later, voilà! Thick, creamy peanut, almond, cashew, sunflower, or hazelnut butter. I prefer using my food processor for this because it's very difficult to get all of that good, hard-earned butter out of the blender jar. I use cashews here, but you can use any type of nut (or seed).

2 cups cashew pieces (your choice, raw, unsalted & roasted, or salted & roasted)
Sea salt, to taste (if using unsalted nuts), optional

▶ Put the nuts and sea salt, if using, into the bowl of a food processor. Process until smooth and glossy. You will need to frequently stop the machine and scrape down the sides. Scrape into an air-tight container and store in the refrigerator indefinitely.

Suggestions
▶ Add a pinch of cinnamon, some maple syrup, or vanilla extract to customize your nut butters.

Gluten-free ▲ Oil-free ▲ Raw Option ▲ Quick ▲ Easy
Total time: **10–12 minutes**

"PARMESAN" CHEEZ

makes about 1 cup

In my house, vegan Parmesan cheese is as ubiquitous as salt is in other households. I use it to enhance the flavor of soups, salad dressings, raw crackers, and of course—pasta. If you have almond meal on hand, you can quickly make up a batch of your own additive-free vegan Parm.

1 cup Almond Meal (see recipe on page 32) or store-bought almond meal
2 Tbsp. lemon juice
2 Tbsp. white miso paste
1 to 2 Tbsp. nutritional yeast

1 tsp. sea salt
1/2 tsp. garlic powder
1/4 tsp. smoked paprika
pinch turmeric

▶ Put all of the ingredients in a food processor and pulse a few times to thoroughly combine. Divide the mixture in two and spread one half on a non-stick dehydrator sheet; do the same with the other half of the mixture.

▶ Set the dehydrator to 115 degrees and dry for about 3 hours, or until the mixture is dry and crumbly. Put mixture in a food processor and pulse to break up any chunks. Put in an air-tight container and store in the refrigerator. Keeps for 7 to 10 days.

Suggestions
▶ Use another kind of nut meal in place of almond meal.
▶ This recipe also works well with the Almond Coconut Meal (see recipe on page 32).
▶ If you don't have a dehydrator, try making this in your oven by setting the oven on its lowest temperature. Bake until the mixture is dry and beginning to brown—about 3 hours. Stir occasionally.

Gluten-free ▲ Oil-free ▲ Raw ▲ Easy
Prep time: **3 hours** *Drying Time:* **8 minutes**

GLUTEN-FREE SWEET PIE CRUST

makes one 9-inch crust

These three pie crusts should take care of most of your pie needs. Both the Whole Wheat Sweet Pie Crust and the Gluten-Free Sweet Pie Crust come out a bit like shortbread—rich, sweet, and firm yet crumbly. I can eat them plain. The raw pie crust is great for raw pudding or cream pies; best part about it is how quickly it comes together—and no need to heat up the oven!

1 cup Gluten-Free All-Purpose Blend (see recipe on page 42)
2 Tbsp. Almond or Almond Coconut Meal (see recipe on page 32)
1 Tbsp. flaxseed meal

1/4 tsp. ground cinnamon
1/4 tsp. powdered stevia
Pinch sea salt
6 Tbsp. tahini
5 Tbsp. Ice water

▶ Add the Gluten-Free All-Purpose Blend, almond meal, flaxseed meal, cinnamon, stevia, and salt to the bowl of a food processor. Pulse a few times to combine. Add the tahini and process until crumbly and combined. With the machine running, drizzle in the ice water. Add just enough until the dough begins to come together. Remove it from the processor and knead a few times and then pat it into a thick round.

▶ Lightly flour a work surface and roll out the dough until it's about ¼ inch thick. Carefully lift it into a 9-inch pie pan and crimp the edges. The crust is now ready to be filled and baked, or blind baked (and then filled).

Suggestions

▶ Substitute your favorite nut butter for some of the tahini.

▶ To blind bake a crust, preheat the oven to 425 degrees. Line the pie pan with parchment paper and fill it with weight—such as dried beans, rice, or coffee beans, taking care that the beans/rice/coffee beans reach all the way to the sides. Bake the crust for about 20 minutes, then remove from the oven and take out the weights and the parchment paper. Bake for an additional 5 minutes to brown up the bottom. If the edge browns too quickly, line with foil.

Gluten-free ▲ Oil-free ▲ Quick ▲ Easy

Total time: **15 minutes**

WHOLE WHEAT SWEET PIE CRUST

makes one 9-inch crust

1 cup whole wheat pastry flour
2 Tbsp. Almond or Almond Coconut
    Meal (see recipe on page 32)
1 Tbsp. flaxseed meal
1/4 tsp. ground cinnamon

1/4 tsp. powdered stevia
Pinch sea salt
6 Tbsp. tahini
5 Tbsp. Ice water

▶ Add the whole wheat pastry flour, almond meal, flaxseed meal, cinnamon, stevia, and salt to the bowl of a food processor. Pulse a few times to combine. Add the tahini and process until crumbly and combined. With the machine running, drizzle in the ice water. Add just enough until the dough begins to come together. Remove it from the processor and knead a few times and then pat it into a thick round.

▶ Lightly flour a work surface and roll out the dough until it's about ¼ inch thick. Carefully lift it into a 9-inch pie pan and crimp the edges. The crust is now ready to be filled and baked, or blind baked (and then filled).

Suggestions

▶ Substitute your favorite nut butter for some of the tahini.

▶ To blind bake a crust, preheat the oven to 425 degrees. Line the pie pan with parchment paper and fill it with weight—such as dried beans, rice, or coffee beans, taking care that the beans/rice/coffee beans reach all the way to the sides. Bake the crust for about 20 minutes, then remove from the oven and take out the weights and the parchment paper. Bake for an additional 5 minutes to brown up the bottom. If the edge browns too quickly, line with foil.

Oil-free ▲ Quick ▲ Easy
Total time: **15 minutes**

RAW PIE CRUST

makes one 9-inch crust

1 cup raw walnuts
1 cup Almond Meal (see recipe on
　　page 32)

5 Medjool dates, pitted and chopped
1/4 cup raw, unsweetened coconut flakes
4 Tbsp. Water

▶ In a food processor, pulse the walnuts until coarsely chopped. Add the almond meal, dates, coconut flakes, and water. Process until a moist dough is formed. Scrape into a 9-inch pie pan and pat the dough along the bottom and up along the sides of the pan. Fill.

Suggestions
▶ Use pecans in place of the walnuts.
▶ It definitely won't be raw anymore, but this crust is delicious when lightly toasted because it brings out the sweetness in the coconut and nuts. I pop it in the toaster oven for 10 to 15 minutes or until lightly browned and fragrant. Keep your eyes on this, however, otherwise you can quickly have an inedible chunk of charcoal instead of crunchy-sweet pie crust.

Gluten Free ▲ Raw ▲ Oil-free ▲ Quick ▲ Easy
Total time: **10 minutes**

VEGETABLE BROTH

makes about 10 cups

The ingredient list is long and roasting the vegetables seems like an added step, but it enhances the flavor of the broth. It doesn't take too long to chop the vegetables—and at the end of the cooking time you'll have fresh broth with which to stock your refrigerator or freezer—and no funky ingredients.

2 large yellow onions, peeled and
    roughly chopped
4 scallions, chopped
1 large carrot, roughly chopped
2 stalks celery, roughly chopped
1 medium-sized turnip, roughly chopped
1 large yellow squash, roughly chopped
1 large zucchini, roughly chopped
4 medium-sized tomatoes, quartered
4 garlic cloves, peeled
1/4 tsp. ground black pepper

4 quarts water
1/2 cup dried porcini mushrooms
4 whole cloves
10 black peppercorns
12 stems fresh thyme, or 2 tsp. dried
1/2 cup fresh parsley leaves and stems or
    2 tsp. dried
8 fresh basil leaves or 1 tsp. dried
1 large stem fresh rosemary, or 2 tsp. dried
1/4 cup tamari or liquid aminos
1/4 cup dry white wine, optional

▶ Preheat the oven to 400 degrees. Place the chopped vegetables on the baking pan and spray lightly with cooking oil. Sprinkle ¼ teaspoon of ground black pepper over top and using your hands, toss the vegetables until all are coated with oil and pepper. Cook the vegetables for 45 minutes, turning occasionally.

▶ Meanwhile, pour the water into a large stock pot. When the vegetables are done, add them to the pot along with the dried mushrooms and spices. Bring the mixture to a boil, then turn down the heat and simmer for 20 minutes. Stir in the tamari and wine, if using. Simmer, partially covered, for an additional 30 minutes.

▶ Let the broth cool and then strain to remove all of the solids. Store the broth in air-tight containers in the refrigerator or freezer.

Suggestions
▶ I've deliberately left this unsalted so that it can be seasoned to taste when used in recipes. Feel free to add additional tamari or sea salt.

Gluten-free ▲ Oil-free ▲ Easy
Total time: **2 hours**

TOFU & CASHEW SOUR CREAM

makes 1 1/2 cups

I just cannot bring myself to purchase vegan sour cream, so over the years I've noodled with making my own. It's quick and easy to do and you decide what goes in it, right? As odd as it sounds, this version uses a crushed vitamin C tablet for added zing. This genius idea came from Bryanna Clark Grogan's book The (Almost) No Fat Cookbook.

1 (12.3-ounce) package extra-firm silken tofu
2 Tbsp. raw cashew pieces, soaked for a few hours, rinsed and drained
1 1/2 Tbsp. fresh lemon juice

1/2 Tbsp. white wine vinegar
1/4 tsp. garlic powder
1/4 tsp. sea salt
1 (1000 mg) vitamin C tablet, crushed, or 1/8 tsp. citric acid

▶ Place all ingredients in a high-speed or regular blender and process until creamy and smooth. Refrigerate for up to 1 week.

Gluten Free ▲ Oil-free ▲ Easy
Total time: **8 minutes**

TEMPEH BACON

makes 16 pieces

I've made this so many times I can practically do it in my sleep—but I never get tired of the salty-smoky flavor. It's lovely on salads, alongside tofu scramble, or tucked in between thick slices of tomato, avocado, and arugula. The 5-Way Chili on page 292 is even tastier with this crumbled on top.

1 (8-ounce) package tempeh, cut into 16 pieces
1/2 cup Vegetable Broth (see recipe on page 60) or store-bought low-sodium broth
1 Tbsp. pure maple syrup
1/4 cup tamari, soy sauce, or liquid aminos
3/4 tsp. ground black pepper
1/2 Tbsp. liquid smoke
1/2 tsp. dried onion flakes
1/4 tsp. smoked paprika
1/4 tsp. garlic powder

▶ Preheat the oven to 425 degrees.
▶ In a 9 × 9 glass baking dish, whisk together everything but the tempeh slices. Add the tempeh slices and turn to coat evenly with the marinade. Let the tempeh rest for about 15 minutes.
▶ Bake the tempeh for 30 to 45 minutes, turning once. If the marinade evaporates, add a splash of vegetable broth and cook for another 5 to 10 minutes. Tempeh should be a deep brown and beginning to crisp at the edges. Serve immediately or store in the refrigerator for up to 1 week.

Suggestions
▶ If you like your bacon thinner, cut the tempeh into 32 slices. Keep in mind that it will cook faster, so watch closely when baking—and you'll need a bigger baking pan.

WHIPPED COCONUT CREAM

makes about 1 cup

When I first tried this easy substitute for dairy whipped cream, the dark clouds parted and I heard the sweet sounds of a heavenly choir. If you've never tried this airy, rich cream dolloped on pumpkin pie or on top of a big scoop of chocolate ice cream, you've been missing out. Put a can of coconut milk in the refrigerator and prepare to be amazed!.

1 (13.5-ounce) can of full-fat unsweetened coconut milk, chilled 8 to 12 hours
5 drops vanilla-flavored stevia liquid, optional, or your favorite sweetener, to taste

▶ Several hours prior to whipping the coconut cream, place a small metal bowl and the metal beaters from a hand mixer in the freezer.

▶ Make sure that you've sufficiently chilled the coconut milk. This step separates the thick coconut cream from the coconut water. Do not shake or turn the can when you remove it from the refrigerator! Open the can and carefully spoon out the white cream that has come to the top of the can—this will be about ⅓ of the can—and put it in the cold metal bowl. Reserve the liquid for another use, such as in smoothies.

▶ Add the stevia or other sweetener, if using, and beat the coconut cream for about 1 minute or until stiff peaks form. That's it! You're done! Serve immediately.

Suggestions

▶ For some reason, not all full-fat coconut milk brands make suitable whipped coconut cream. It's really just a matter of trial and error to find the brand that whips up the way that you like it. The brand I use is Native Forest Organic and it whips up very quickly and with a lovely velvety consistency that stays firm even a few days later.

▶ Chilling the bowl and beaters is a little trick I learned from my mother. From exhaustive and dedicated research, mom discovered that a cold bowl and icy beaters help the cream to thicken faster—probably because the cold metal quickly solidifies the fat in the milk. This step isn't necessary, but if mom does it, that's all I need to know.

▶ For my tastes, sweetener really isn't needed at all, but it does bump up the special-ness of this cream. And I suggest vanilla flavoring here simply for folks who are not overly fond of the flavor of coconut. Skip it if you are a coconut cream purist.

Gluten-free ▲ Oil-free ▲ Quick ▲ Easy

Prep time: **8 hours, to chill coconut milk** *Cook time:* **2 minutes**

The Kiwanis Club's annual pancake breakfast.
Warm toast showered with cinnamon and sugar.
A baguette in a bicycle basket.
Dr. Atkins's worst nightmare.
Crusty, airy, yeasty, toothsome.
Carbs.

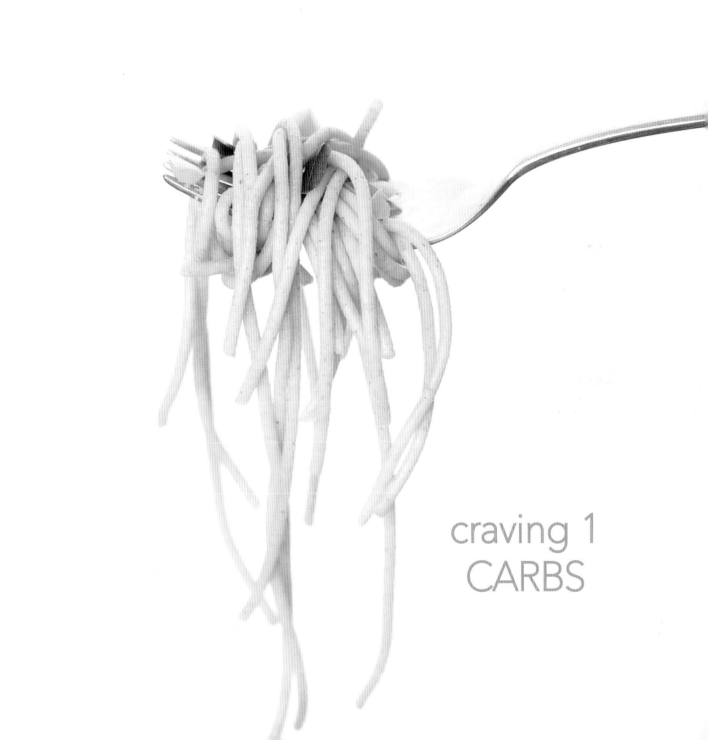

craving 1
CARBS

BUCKWHEAT "BLACK BREAD"

makes 12 pieces

Looking for a way to recreate the flavors of dark rye bread without gluten, I came up with this hearty, raw cracker. It's delicious spread with Cashew Coconut Cream Cheez on page 36, or with the Roasted Garlic & Fresh Herb Cream Cheez on page 164.

1 cup buckwheat groats, soaked 8 to 12 hours, rinsed and drained
1 cup raw walnuts, soaked 8 to 12 hours, rinsed and drained
1/4 cup water
2 cloves garlic
1/4 cup red onion, chopped
1 tsp. lemon juice

1 Tbsp. pure maple syrup
1/4 cup flaxseed meal
1 Tbsp. cacao or cocoa powder
1 Tbsp. caraway seeds
1/2 tsp. powdered herbal coffee substitute (such as Cafix or Dandy Blend), optional
1/4 tsp. ground black pepper

▷ In the bowl of a food processor, pulse the buckwheat and walnuts to break them up. Add the water, garlic, red onion, lemon juice, and maple syrup and process until smooth.

▷ Scrape mixture into a large bowl. Add the flaxseed meal, cacao or cocoa powder, caraway seeds, coffee substitute, and black pepper and stir until thoroughly combined.

▷ Spread the mixture onto a non-stick dehydrator sheet to about ¼ inch thick. Gently score the dough into large rectangles or squares.

▷ Dehydrate at 115 degrees for 8 to 10 hours or until the desired crispiness is achieved. Carefully break the bread apart and store pieces in an air-tight container for up to 10 days.

Suggestions

▷ After 2 to 3 hours in the dehydrator, carefully flip the bread by placing a mesh dehydrator sheet fitted into another tray on top of the dough. Flip and gently peel away the non-stick sheet. Place the tray back in the dehydrator to continue drying. This will speed up the dehydrating time.

Gluten-free ▲ Oil-free ▲ Raw ▲ Easy

Prep time: **10 minutes** *Cook time:* **22-24 hours**

Carbs

CAULIFLOWER, POTATO, & PICKLE WRAPS WITH TAHINI DRESSING

makes 4 to 6 wraps

If you're familiar with the television show Seinfeld, *then you probably remember the episode about "The Bad Breaker-Upper." Well, I'm "The Bad Wrapper-Upper." I can't roll a wrap or burrito to save my life! But it doesn't stop me from trying.*

This recipe was inspired by one I saw many years ago on a blog called Herbivoress, *and I was surprised at how delicious this seemingly strange combination of flavors was. My recipe is admittedly a lot more complicated than the original—but the basics are there: potato, cauliflower, tahini, and pickles.*

Filling

1 large baking potato, peeled and cut into 1/2-inch cubes
4 cups chopped cauliflower
1 small onion, diced
4 cloves garlic, roughly chopped
1/2 cup Vegetable Broth (see page 60 for recipe), or store-bought low-sodium vegetable broth
2 Tbsp. liquid aminos or tamari
1 tsp. cumin powder
1 tsp. garlic powder
1/2 tsp. ground black pepper
1/4 tsp. ground coriander
Pinch sea salt
Pinch cayenne
Pinch sweet paprika
2 cups finely chopped romaine lettuce
2 Tbsp. chopped fresh parsley
4 kosher dill pickle spears
4 whole wheat or gluten-free tortillas, lavash, or pita

Dressing

1/2 cup tahini
1 clove garlic
2 Tbsp. to 1/4 cup apple cider vinegar
1/4 cup water
1 Tbsp. fresh lemon juice
1/2 to 1 Tbsp. white miso paste
1 tsp. dried onion flakes
1/2 tsp. cumin powder
1/4 tsp. ground black pepper
Pinch cayenne

▶ Preheat the oven to 425 degrees. In a large bowl, combine the potato, cauliflower, onion, garlic, vegetable broth, liquid aminos, and spices and toss to combine. Pour this mixture into a shallow baking dish and spread into one layer to speed cooking.

▶ Bake the potato-cauliflower mixture for about 45 minutes, turning the vegetables two or three times. The vegetables should be soft and slightly browned at the edges. If the mixture dries out during the cooking time, add a splash or two of water or vegetable broth.

▶ While the vegetables cook, prepare the dressing. Combine all of the dressing ingredients in a high-speed or regular blender and process until very smooth. Set aside.

▶ To serve, gently warm the tortillas, lavash, or pita breads. You can either mix the vegetables with the dressing, or you can spread some of the tahini dressing on/into the breads and then add the other ingredients on top. Divide the romaine lettuce between the breads, then spoon on the potato-cauliflower mixture, sprinkle with chopped parsley and top with one pickle spear per wrap.

Suggestions
▶ I prefer to eat this when the potato-cauliflower mixture is warm, rather than hot.

Gluten-free option ▲ Oil-free ▲ Easy
Total time: **1 hour 15 minutes, including roasting time**

COCOA-CINNAMON FRENCH TOAST

serves 4

To me this is the ultimate brunch dish: rich, a bit decadent and a little more special than the standard pancakes, waffles, or French toast. My default nut butter to use is peanut butter, but experiment with your favorite kind—and feel free to switch up the fruit, too—or slather on some Cherry-Pomegranate Refrigerator Jam on page 276.

Coating
3/4 cup water
1/2 cup raw cashew pieces, soaked for a few hours, rinsed and drained
1 Tbsp. cacao or cocoa powder
1 tsp. chickpea flour
1/2 tsp. ground cinnamon
1/2 tsp. vanilla extract
1/4 tsp. maca powder, optional
6 to 8 drops vanilla-flavored liquid stevia

French toast
8 thin slices of Vanilla Cardamom Quickbread (see recipe on page 85) or whole wheat or gluten-free bread

Optional toppings
Banana slices
Strawberries, thinly sliced
Nut butter
Chocolate Syrup (see recipe on page 93)
Whipped Coconut Cream (see recipe on page 64)

- -

▶ In a high-speed or regular blender, process all of the coating ingredients until very smooth. Pour the mixture into a shallow baking dish and set aside.

▶ Heat a large pan or electric skillet over medium heat. Lightly spritz the pan/skillet with oil. Dip the bread slices in the coating and shake gently to remove excess.

▶ Cook for about 5 minutes on one side, flip and cook for an additional 4 to 5 minutes. The toast should be a deep brown and crusty. Keep French toast warm in a 200 degree oven while you prepare the remaining slices.

▶ Serve with some of the suggested toppings, or your favorites.

▶ You can prepare the coating the night before, but you may need to thin it with a little water before dipping the bread.

▶ It's not necessary, but I always let my bread slices rest on a cooling rack overnight to dry just a little. I think this step makes them sturdier for dipping and grilling.

Gluten-free option

DIANNE'S GREEN & WHITE PIZZA

makes one pizza

This hearty and satisfying pizza has everything: chewy crust, creamy ricotta, garlicky pesto and a generous helping of cruciferous veggies in the form of cauliflower and broccoli, both of which provide you with calcium, vitamin C, and vitamin K.

Cashew Ricotta
1 cup raw cashews, soaked in water for two hours, rinsed and drained
1 Tbsp. lemon juice
1 Tbsp. nutritional yeast
1/4 tsp. sea salt
3 Tbsp. water

Spinach Pesto
1 (5-ounce) package baby spinach
1/2 cup raw cashews, soaked in water for two hours, rinsed and drained
2 cloves garlic
2 Tbsp. nutritional yeast
1 Tbsp. lemon juice
1 tsp. mellow white miso paste
1/4 tsp. sea salt

2 Tbsp. Vegetable Broth (see recipe on page 60) or store-bought low-sodium broth

For the Pizza
1 Tbsp. olive oil
2 cups broccoli, chopped into bite-sized pieces
2 cups cauliflower, chopped into bite-sized pieces
1/4 tsp. sea salt
1/4 teaspoon black pepper
1 recipe Multigrain Pizza Dough (see recipe on pages 50 and 51)
1/4 cup kalamata olives, chopped
1/4 cup sun-dried (not oil-packed) tomatoes, sliced into thin ribbons

- -

Make the Ricotta
▶ Process all of the ricotta ingredients in a food processor until fluffy. This could take 5 to 10 minutes. You will need to stop the food processor and scrape down the sides with a spatula a few times.

Make the Spinach Pesto
▶ Combine the spinach, cashews, nutritional yeast, lemon juice, miso paste, and sea salt in a food processor. Process until ingredients are chopped and just slightly chunky. While the motor is running, drizzle in the vegetable broth. Continue to mix until well combined.

Make the Pizza

▶ Preheat oven to 400 degrees. Toss the broccoli and cauliflower in the olive oil and sprinkle with salt and pepper. Place on a roasting pan and cook for 15 to 20 minutes, turning the vegetables over once about halfway through.

▶ Spread the pesto evenly over the crust. Use a spoon to drop the cashew ricotta on top of the pesto, flattening the dollops out a little with the back of the spoon. Spread the broccoli, cauliflower, olives, and sun-dried tomatoes evenly over the top of the pizza.

▶ Turn the oven up to 500 degrees. Bake the pizza for 5 to 10 minutes, until heated throughout.

Suggestions

▶ Soak sun-dried tomatoes in water for 15 minutes if they are too dry to slice.
▶ To make this oil-free, roast the broccoli and cauliflower in some water or vegetable broth.

Oil-free option

GLUTEN-FREE PUMPKIN CHAI WAFFLES

makes 3 large waffles

In my opinion, there are two key steps in guaranteeing crisp and delicious waffles. The first is to warm the plates on which the waffles will be served. I do this by setting oven-safe plates in a 200-degree oven while I prepare the waffles. The second is to place the cooked waffles in the warm oven directly on the rack. This not only keeps the waffles toasty-warm while you prepare the rest of them, but that beautiful crispness on the outside of the waffle will be retained. Heated plates assure the waffles will be nice and warm through-out breakfast.

2 cups Gluten-Free All-Purpose Flour
   Blend (see recipe on page 42)
2 Tbsp. flaxseed meal
2 tsp. baking powder
1/2 tsp. sea salt
1/2 tsp. powdered stevia
1/2 tsp. cinnamon
1/2 tsp. ground ginger
1/4 tsp. baking soda

1/4 tsp anise seeds ground in a coffee/
   spice grinder
1/4 tsp. ground cardamom
1/4 tsp. cloves or allspice
Pinch ground black pepper
1 3/4 cups non-dairy milk mixed with 1
   tsp. apple cider vinegar
1/2 cup pumpkin purée
1 tsp. vanilla extract

▶ In a large bowl, whisk together the flour, flaxseed meal, baking powder, salt, baking soda, stevia, and spices. Set aside.

▶ In a small bowl, whisk together the non-dairy milk/apple cider vinegar mixture, pumpkin, and vanilla extract. Pour this mixture into the dry ingredients and whisk well to combine. Make sure there are no lumps. Let the batter rest for 15 minutes while you heat the waffle iron.

▶ When the waffle iron is ready, lightly spray it with cooking oil. Ladle a generous amount of batter onto the center of the waffle iron and spread it out, leaving about ½ inch of waffle iron—this gives the batter space to spread when pressed. Cook for about 6 minutes and then gently lift the waffle from the iron and place it on an oven rack.

▶ When all of the batter has been used, serve the waffles with your favorite toppings.

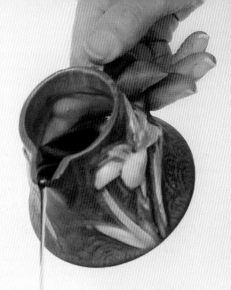

Suggestions

▶ The yield depends on the size of your waffle maker.

▶ This recipe can be made with wheat-based flour as well.

▶ This recipe can be used for pancakes, but you will need to add more liquid to the batter.

Gluten-free ▲ Oil-free ▲ Easy

KATHY'S WHOLE WHEAT VEGGIE QUINOA DROP BISCUITS

makes about 12 biscuits

Biscuits are the perfect accompaniment to warming stews and soups because unlike yeast breads, no kneading is required and you can whip up a batch right before dinner. Biscuits also freeze well. Individually wrap the extras, freeze and re-heat them in the oven for when you need a quick side or bread for a veggie sandwich.

Kathy pumps up the nutritional value of these drop biscuits by adding kale, carrots, and quinoa.

1 1/2 tsp. apple cider vinegar or white vinegar
3/4 cup soy milk
1 Tbsp. Vegetable Broth (see recipe on page 60) or store-bought low-sodium vegetable broth
1/2 cup finely grated carrot
1 1/2 cups finely minced kale or other green
1 cup cooked quinoa
2 cups whole wheat pastry flour
2 tsp. baking powder
1/2 tsp. baking soda
1/2 tsp. salt
1/2 cup refined coconut oil

- ▶ Preheat the oven to 350 degrees. Add the apple cider vinegar to the measuring cup with the soy milk and set aside.
- ▶ Heat the vegetable broth in a pan over medium heat and add the kale. Sauté for 1 to 3 minutes or until it turns bright green. Pour into a large bowl with the carrots and quinoa. Set aside.
- ▶ In a food processor, add the whole wheat pastry flour and process for about 2 minutes to make it finer and the biscuits a little lighter. Add baking powder, baking soda, and salt and process for about 1 minute to mix everything together thoroughly.
- ▶ Next, add the coconut oil to the food processor about 2 tablespoons at a time and pulse for 30 seconds to a minute each time. At the end of the process, the mixture will start to look like coarse cornmeal. If there are a few teaspoon-sized lumps of oil, don't worry, they will mix in later.
- ▶ Pour the flour mixture into the large bowl with the veggies, quinoa and soy milk-vinegar mixture. Mix well with a wooden spoon to spread the veggies throughout the mixture and to smash up any oil pieces that remain.

Oliverio

- Line a baking sheet with parchment or lightly spray with oil. Using a ¼ cup measure, form about 12 biscuits. They will be domed from the scoop, but if you don't like that you can flatten them with the palm of your hand. They will not spread out during cooking.
- Cook for about 13 to 17 minutes, or until they turn light brown on the bottoms.

Suggestions

- The batter is very wet. Dip the ¼ cup measure in water to scoop up batter. Turn over and tap gently to release onto baking sheet.
- Use vegan butter in place of the coconut oil, if preferred.
- You can use any non-dairy milk, but only soy will get thick after the vinegar is added.

ORANGE PECAN MINI BANANA BREADS

makes 4 mini loaves

I could happily eat banana bread in almost any way, shape or form every single day of the week. It's my favorite way to use up bananas that over-ripen before I can use them.

1 1/2 cups Gluten-Free All-Purpose Blend (see recipe on page 42)
1/4 cup gluten-free rolled oats
1 Tbsp. baking powder
1 1/2 tsp. cinnamon
1 tsp. powdered stevia or 1 Tbsp. pure maple syrup
1/2 tsp. guar gum or xanthan gum, optional
1/2 tsp. sea salt
1/4 tsp. ground cardamom
1/4 tsp. ground ginger

3 large, very ripe bananas
1/2 cup Date Paste (see recipe on page 40)
1/4 cup coconut oil, softened or melted
2 Tbsp. chia seeds mixed with 1/4 cup orange juice or water
1 Tbsp. apple cider vinegar
1 tsp. vanilla extract
1/2 tsp. orange oil, optional
Zest of 1 orange
1 cup chopped pecans

▶ Preheat the oven to 350 degrees and place 4 lightly-oiled 1-cup mini loaf pans on a large baking sheet.
▶ In a large bowl, whisk together the flours, rolled oats, cinnamon, baking powder, stevia, guar gum, sea salt, cardamom, and ginger. Set aside.
▶ In a medium-sized bowl, mash the bananas and then stir in the date paste, coconut oil, chia seed mixture, apple cider vinegar, vanilla extract, orange oil, and orange zest. When thoroughly combined, add this to the flour mixture and stir well. Fold in the chopped pecans.
▶ Divide the batter between the four mini loaf pans and bake for about 30 minutes. Place the loaves on a cooling rack and let cool slightly before removing them from the pans.

Suggestions
▶ Add a ½ cup of stevia-sweetened semi-sweet chocolate chips.
▶ If you prefer, bake the banana bread in a 9 × 5 loaf pan, but be sure to bake it longer—about 1 hour.
▶ Substitute 2 tablespoons flaxseed meal for the chia seeds if you don't like the slight crunch of the chia seeds.

Gluten-free ▲ Easy

POP'S PASTA BROCCOLINI

serves 4

Though my mom did most of the cooking in our household, Dad (or Pops, as I call him) is an excellent cook in his own right with some impressive improvisational skills and delicious recipes that became family traditions, especially on holidays. One of our favorites was something we called broccolini. Long before anyone had ever heard of the broccoli-kale hybrid called broccolini, we were eating this rich pasta loaded with steamed broccoli and smothered in a rich garlicky-lemon-cream sauce.

4 cups broccoli, cut into bite-sized pieces
1 (13.25-ounces) package gluten-free
    pasta (shells, penne, rotini)
3/4 cup raw cashew pieces, soaked for a
    few hours, rinsed and drained
1/2 cup Vegetable Broth (see recipe
    on page 60) or store-bought low-
    sodium broth
2 Tbsp. fresh lemon juice
1 Tbsp. liquid aminos

1/4 cup silken tofu
2 cloves garlic
2 tsp. nutritional yeast
1/4 tsp. ground black pepper
Zest of 1 lemon
"Parmesan" Cheez (see recipe on page
    54), for sprinkling on top of the
    pasta, optional
Fresh basil, for garnish, optional

▶ Fill a large pot with water and toss in a large pinch of kosher salt. Bring the water to a boil and lightly cook the broccoli until crisp-tender, 3 to 4 minutes. Remove the broccoli with a slotted spoon, rinse with cool water and set aside. With the water at a boil, add the pasta and cook according to package directions.

▶ While the pasta cooks, make the sauce by combining the cashews, vegetable broth, lemon juice, liquid aminos, tofu, garlic, nutritional yeast, and black pepper in a high-speed or regular blender. Process until very smooth, 30 seconds to 1 minute. Pour the mixture into a small saucepan, stir in the lemon zest and warm the sauce over low heat. Stir occasionally and add more vegetable broth or water if the mixture becomes too thick.

▶ Drain the pasta and put it back in the pot. Mix in the sauce and the broccoli and stir well to combine. Divide the pasta between four deep bowls and sprinkle with Parmesan Cheez and fresh basil, if using.

Suggestions
- ▶ Use your favorite vegetables instead of, or in combination with, the broccoli.
- ▶ For extra green and nutrition, stir in 2 cups baby spinach leaves when you add the broccoli and sauce; cover the pot for a few minutes, or until spinach has wilted slightly.
- ▶ Top with Salty & Sweet Marinated Baked Mushrooms (see page 232 for recipe)
- ▶ Add a dash of red pepper flakes to the sauce, if desired.
- ▶ When reheating leftovers, add a splash of hot water or vegetable broth and stir to loosen the sauce.
- ▶ Add slices of vegan Italian sausage.

Gluten-free ▲ Oil-free ▲ Easy

Prep time: **20 minutes** *Cook time:* **about 15 minutes**

VANILLA CARDAMOM QUICKBREAD

makes one loaf

I made this loaf to be used in the Cocoa-Cinnamon French Toast on page 72, but it's good in its own right. The flavors are mild and the sweetness very light so that it doesn't overwhelm the chocolate in the toast. Increase the amount of sweetness, if you like. Maple syrup can be used as a sweetener (about ½ cup), but you'll probably want to eliminate the non-dairy milk.

2 cups whole wheat pastry flour
1 Tbsp. maca powder, optional
1 1/2 tsp. powdered stevia
1 tsp. ground cardamom
1/2 tsp. ground ginger
1 1/2 tsp. baking powder
1/2 tsp. baking soda
Pinch salt
1 cup pumpkin purée

1/2 cup Tofu & Cashew Sour Cream (see recipe on page 61) or store-bought vegan sour cream
1/4 cup non-dairy milk
1/4 cup refined coconut oil
1/4 cup tahini
2 tsp. vanilla extract
1 tsp. vanilla-flavored liquid stevia
1/2 cup chopped pecans or walnuts

▶ Preheat the oven to 350 degrees and lightly oil an 8 × 4 loaf pan.
▶ In a medium-sized bowl, whisk together the flour, maca, stevia, cardamom, baking powder, baking soda, and salt. Set aside.
▶ In the bowl of a stand-mixer, mix the pumpkin purée, sour cream, non-dairy milk, coconut oil, tahini, vanilla extract, vanilla stevia, and pecans or walnuts. Carefully add the flour mixture and stir until thoroughly combined.
▶ Scrape the batter into the prepared pan and bake the loaf for 50 to 60 minutes. It should be cracked and browned on the top and be firm to the touch. Let the bread cool in the pan for 15 minutes, then remove loaf and let it cool completely on a wire rack.

Suggestions
▶ You can also use unsweetened plain non-dairy yogurt in place of the vegan sour cream.

Easy

Total time: **1 hour 10 minutes**

WHOLE WHEAT PEACH PANCAKES

makes about 15 pancakes

My weekend isn't complete without a crispy waffle or a warm stack of pancakes—almost always smothered in nut butter and banana slices. I complete this breakfast with fresh juice (usually beet-apple-ginger-carrot) and a big mug of chai tea. Needless to say, I'm completely satisfied and stuffed until . . . lunchtime!
These are super-simple pancakes with a basic batter that is adaptable to all kinds of variations—add cinnamon, use pumpkin purée instead of yogurt, go chocolatey with some cocoa powder, and/or stir in chopped nuts or grated apple.

2 cups whole wheat flour
2 Tbsp. wheat germ
2 tsp. baking soda
1 tsp. baking powder
1 tsp. ground ginger
1/2 tsp. powdered stevia
1 3/4 cups non-dairy milk

1/4 cup plain non-dairy yogurt
1 heaping Tbsp. fresh ginger, grated or
    finely minced
1 tsp. vanilla extract
3 ripe peaches, pitted and chopped
    (about 2 cups)

▷ Preheat the oven to 200 degrees and place your plates inside to warm up.
▷ In a large mixing bowl, whisk together the whole wheat flour, wheat germ, baking soda, baking powder, ginger, and stevia.
▷ In a small bowl, whisk together the non-dairy milk, yogurt, ginger, and vanilla extract. Add this to the flour mixture and whisk to thoroughly combine. Fold in the chopped peaches. Let the batter sit for about 15 minutes while you heat up a griddle or skillet.
▷ When the griddle is hot, lightly spray it with cooking oil. Ladle on about ¼ to ⅓ cup of batter for each pancake, gently spreading it into a circle. Cook the pancakes for 2 to 3 minutes or until the edges begin to firm, then flip and cook an additional 2 to 3 minutes. Remove the pancakes from the griddle and place them on a wire rack. Place the wire rack in the oven so that the pancakes stay warm while you make the rest.
▷ Serve with additional chopped peaches and maple syrup—or your favorite pancake toppings.

Suggestions

▶ You can also reserve the peaches rather than folding them into the batter. As you form the batter into pancakes on the griddle, place 4 to 5 pieces of peach on each pancake. Cook, flip, and cook as above. Sasha, one of my recipe testers, noted that she got 9 pancakes when adding the fruit to the formed pancakes rather than folding it in.

▶ You can use frozen peaches. Let them completely thaw out in the refrigerator the night before you make the pancakes. Chop and be sure to drain any liquid before adding the peaches to the pancake batter.

Oil-free ▲ Easy
Total time: **30–40 minutes**

Tearing into the brown wrapper and shiny, crinkly foil;
the sharp snap and the brittle-sweet bite.
The slow, luscious slide of hot fudge avalanching
down snowy drifts of vanilla ice cream.
The hidden treasures in Easter baskets
and Christmas stockings.
Deep, dark, drippy, melty.
Chocolate.

craving 2
CHOCOLATE

BLUEBERRY CHOCOLATE ANTI-INFLAMMATORY SHAKE

serves 2 to 3

When I started experiencing joint and muscle pain, I researched foods with anti-inflammatory properties and experimented with different recipes to come up with one beverage that had a whole slew of anti-inflammatory ingredients. I was thrilled to learn that chocolate made the list!

2 cups frozen blueberries
2 cups green tea, chilled
1 avocado, pitted and peeled or 1
    banana
5 Medjool dates, chopped

1 Tbsp. cacao or cocoa powder
1/2 tsp. ground cinnamon
1/4 tsp. ground turmeric
Liquid stevia, to taste, or your favorite
    sweetener to taste

▶ Put all ingredients except for the stevia in a high-speed or regular blender. Process until very smooth. Taste and add stevia or other sweetener to taste.

Suggestions
▶ If you do not have a high-speed blender, you may wish to soak the dates for a few hours prior to preparing this smoothie.
▶ If you use the banana instead of the avocado, the smoothie will be sweeter, but less thick.
▶ Add up to 1 cup mild-tasting greens, if desired.

Gluten-free ▲ Oil-free ▲ Quick ▲ Easy
Total time: **8 minutes**

CHOCOLATE HEMPCHATA

serves 2 to 3

A slightly-different take on the refreshing classic Mexican beverage—usually made with rice and without chocolate—that is perfect for warm weather comfort.

2 cups chilled hemp seed milk (homemade or store-bought, just be sure it's unsweetened)
1 cup ice cubes
5 Tbsp. Date Paste (see recipe on page 40), or your favorite sweetener, to taste
3 Tbsp. cacao or cocoa powder
1 1/4 tsp. ground cinnamon
1 tsp. vanilla extract
Tiny pinch sea salt, optional

▶ Put all ingredients in a high-speed or regular blender and process until smooth. Taste and adjust for sweetness.

Suggestions
▶ To make your own hemp milk, put ½ cup hemp seeds and 3 cups water in a blender and process. If desired, strain through a nut milk bag or a fine-meshed sieve. Yield is about 2½ cups.
▶ To simplify this recipe even further, put ½ cup hemp seeds and 2½ cups water along with the ice cubes, dates paste, cocoa powder, cinnamon, vanilla, and sea salt, process and drink!

Gluten-free ▲ Oil-free ▲ Raw ▲ Quick ▲ Easy
Total time: **5 minutes**

EASY CHOCOLATE SAUCE

makes 1 cup

As a kid, I was addicted to Hershey's chocolate syrup—which used to come in a can wrapped tantalizingly in dark brown paper, hinting at the lusciousness inside. I would pour a big shiny dollop into a glass of cold milk or drizzle it over ice cream. It's so easy to make a healthful version—one that you can sweeten to your tastes. Stir a couple of tablespoons of this into a glass of homemade non-dairy milk and you'll be transported back to childhood.

Why do I use both date paste and stevia? You don't have to, but I found that the date paste added an almost smoky flavor and contributed to the texture of the final product. Feel free to sweeten it entirely with stevia if you wish.

1 cup non-dairy milk
2 Tbsp. Date Paste (see recipe on page 40)
1 Tbsp. herbal coffee substitute powder (such as Cafix or Dandy Blend), optional
1/4 cup cacao or cocoa powder

1/4 cup vegan stevia-sweetened semi-sweet chocolate chips
1 tsp. kuzu powder mixed with 2 tsp. cool water
1/4 to 1/2 tsp. vanilla-flavored stevia liquid

▶ In a small saucepan, warm the non-dairy milk and whisk in the date paste, cacao or cocoa powder, and chocolate chips. When the chocolate chips have melted, whisk in the kuzu-water mixture and stir until mixture has thickened slightly, about 2 minutes.

▶ Remove pan from the heat and stir in the stevia. Store leftovers in an air-tight container for up to 1 week.

Gluten-free ▲ Oil-free ▲ Quick ▲ Easy
Total time: **10 minutes**

COCO-NUTTY CHOCOLATE CHIP COOKIES, RAW OR BAKED

makes 8

If you take the baked route, these cookies are almost instant gratification for a sweet chocolate craving. Either baked or raw, you don't have to wrestle with a lot of guilt when eating these sugar-free, oil-free, and grain-free treats.

1 cup walnuts
6 Medjool dates, pitted and chopped
1/2 cup unsweetened applesauce
1/4 cup almond butter
1 tsp. vanilla extract
Pinch sea salt
1/2 cup flaxseed meal
1/4 cup unsweetened coconut flakes
(use the small shreds, not the large flakes)
1/2 tsp. baking soda (for the baked version ONLY)
1/3 cup stevia-sweetened semi-sweet vegan chocolate chips or regular semi-sweet vegan chocolate chips

---

▶ Add the walnuts and dates to the bowl of a food processor and pulse a few times just to break them into smaller chunks. Add the applesauce, almond butter, vanilla extract and salt and process until mostly smooth—but to the point where you can still see small pieces of walnuts.

▶ In a large bowl, whisk together the flaxseed meal and the coconut flakes—and the baking soda only if you are baking the cookies. Scrape the walnut-date mixture into the flaxseed meal mixture and stir thoroughly. You don't want to have any clumps of dry flaxseed meal. Stir in the chocolate chips.

To bake the cookies

▶ Preheat the oven to 350 degrees. Line a baking sheet with parchment paper or a silicone mat and using a ¼ cup measure, scoop up some dough, pat it down into the measuring cup and then tap the cup on the palm of your hand so that the dough falls out. Place it on the parchment paper, flatten and neaten up the edges. The cookies should be about 1½ to 2 inches in diameter. Continue with the remaining dough. Bake for 10 minutes and then carefully flip the cookies over and bake for an additional five minutes. The cookies should be firm but still feel soft. Let them cool on the pan for a few minutes before placing them on a cooling rack. Store in an air-tight container.

Oliverio

To dehydrate the cookies

▶ Line a dehydrator tray with a non-stick sheet. Use a ¼ cup measure to scoop up some dough, then pat it down into the measuring cup and tap the cup on the palm of your hand so that the dough falls out. Place it on the non-stick sheet, flatten and neaten up the edges. The cookies should be about 1½ to 2 inches in diameter. Continue with the remaining dough. Dehydrate the cookies at 115 degrees for 7 to 8 hours or until firm yet still soft. About three hours into dehydrating, gently place the cookies onto a mesh sheet to speed up the drying process. Eat warm out of the dehydrator and store leftovers in an air-tight container.

Gluten-free ▲ Oil-free
Raw Option ▲ Easy

DOUBLE CHOCOLATE BERRY GOOD COOKIES

makes about 18

One of my recipe testers told me that both she and her mother thought these cookies had a good "flavor profile." I interpreted that to mean that they were satisfyingly chocolatey without a lot of guilt. High in fiber, protein, vitamin C, and vitamin A, bright red Goji berries also contain selenium, zinc, iron, and calcium. Beautiful blueberries have fiber, are low in calories, but high in protective antioxidants that block the activity of free radicals, which may be a factor in the development of cancer.

1 Tbsp. flaxseed meal whisked into 3 Tbsp. water
1/4 Coconut Butter (see recipe on page 37)
1/4 cup pure maple syrup
1 very ripe banana
1 tsp. vanilla extract
Pinch sea salt
1 cup gluten-free oat flour
1/2 cup cocoa or cacao powder

1 Tbsp. arrowroot powder
1 1/2 tsp. stevia powder
1/2 tsp. baking powder
1/2 tsp. baking soda
1/2 tsp. cinnamon
Dash cardamom powder
3/4 cup vegan stevia-sweetened semi-sweet chocolate chips
1/4 cup dried blueberries
1/4 cup dried goji berries

▶ Preheat oven to 375 degrees and line two baking sheets with silicone mats or parchment paper. In a small bowl, whisk together the flaxseed meal and the water and set aside. Put the blueberries and goji berries in a small bowl and cover with warm water for about 15 minutes to rehydrate. Drain and set aside.

▶ In the bowl of a stand mixer, cream together the coconut butter, maple syrup, banana, vanilla extract, salt and flaxseed meal mixture. Process until very smooth.

▶ In a medium-sized bowl, whisk together the oat flour, cocoa or cacao powder, arrowroot powder, stevia, baking powder, baking soda, cinnamon, and cardamom. Carefully pour into the bowl with the coconut butter mixture and process at medium-low speed to incorporate the dry ingredients fully into the wet ingredients. Add the chocolate chips, blueberries, and goji berries and pulse to blend into the cookie dough. The dough will be very sticky.

▶ Drop dough by the heaped tablespoon onto the prepared baking sheets. Flatten and shape slightly. Bake for 10 to 12 minutes, switching pans halfway through for even baking. Let cookies cool on the pan for about 10 minutes before removing them and placing them on cooling racks.

Suggestions
▶ Make your own oat flour by pulsing rolled oats in a food processor or mini prep until finely pulverized. For one cup oat flour you'll need about 1¼ cups rolled oats.

Gluten-free ▲ Oil-free
Total time: 30–40 minutes

MALTED CHOCOLATE–ORANGE SMOOTHIE

serves 2 to 3

1 cup "Malted" Milk (see recipe on page 160)
2 bananas, cut into chunks
1 tsp. orange zest
2 oranges, peeled and cut into chunks
2 Tbsp. cacao or cocoa powder

1 Tbsp. Date Paste (see recipe on page 40)
1 Tbsp. maca powder, optional
2 to 3 ice cubes
2 cups beet greens

▶ Put all ingredients in a high-speed blender and process until smooth and creamy.

Suggestions
▶ Use coconut water, water, or plain non-dairy milk instead of "Malted" Milk.
▶ Use your favorite sweetener to taste instead of Date Paste.
▶ Use spinach or kale in place of beet greens.

Gluten-free ▲ Oil-free ▲ Raw ▲ Quick ▲ Easy
Total time: **about 5 minutes**

MINT CHOCOLATE CHOCOLATE CHIP POPSICLES

makes 6

Another childhood favorite of mine was Jell-O chocolate pudding pops. My grown-up version uses whole food ingredients with a little nutritional boost from cacao and fresh mint.

1 1/8 cup full-fat coconut milk
1/2 cup silken tofu
1/2 cup fresh mint leaves
1/4 cup vegan stevia-sweetened semi-
    sweet chocolate chips, melted

3 Tbsp. cocoa or cacao powder
3 Tbsp. pure maple syrup, or to taste
2 to 3 drops peppermint extract
1/4 cup cacao nibs, optional

▶ Combine all ingredients in a blender and process until very smooth. Add the cacao nibs, if using, and pulse the blender a few times to incorporate.
▶ Divide the mixture between 6 popsicle molds (each mold holding about 4 ounces each). You want to leave about ¼ inch of room at the top of the mold because the mixture will expand as it freezes. Freeze for 4 to 5 hours or until solid. To remove the popsicles from the mold, run the molds briefly under warm water.

Suggestions
▶ The number of popsicles you get will depend on the size of your molds. Follow your particular mold's directions for filling and freezing. I use Metro brand stainless steel molds.

Gluten-free ▲ Oil-free ▲ Easy

MYSTICAL MINT COOKIES

makes 12 sandwich cookies

When I was a kid, my favorite cookie was something called a Mystic Mint. It was an Oreo filled with minty-cream and coated in dark chocolate. Yeah. I believe that it's no longer made, and anyway, it had ingredients that I no longer consume. Making a high-raw version with more wholesome ingredients was my goal. Although these are healthier than the original, consider these chocolatey cookies a rare treat rather than a daily snack.

This recipe takes a little more time and effort than your average cookie, but they are well worth it.

Cookies
1/2 cup flaxseed meal
1/4 cup cacao powder
1 Tbsp. herbal coffee substitute powder, such as Cafix or Dandy Blend
1 cup raw walnuts
1/4 raw sunflower seeds
1/4 cup cacao nibs
1/4 cup Date Paste (see recipe on page 40)
2 Tbsp. Easy Chocolate Sauce (see recipe on page 93) or a stevia-sweetened chocolate syrup, such as NuNaturals brand
1/2 cup water

Mint Cream
1/4 cup lightly packed fresh mint leaves
1/4 cup coconut oil
1/2 cup raw cashews, soaked 8 to 12 hours, rinsed and drained
1 tsp. peppermint-flavored stevia liquid
3 Tbsp. non-dairy milk

Chocolate-Mint Coating
1 (9-ounce) package of vegan stevia-sweetened semi-sweet chocolate chips
10 drops peppermint-flavored liquid stevia
1 tsp. coconut oil
Cacao nibs, for decoration, optional

Make the cookies
▶ In a large bowl, whisk together the flaxseed meal, cacao powder, and herbal coffee substitute. Set aside.
▶ In the bowl of a food processor, combine the walnuts and sunflower seeds. Pulse to break down into small pieces. Add the date paste, chocolate syrup, cacao nibs, and water. Process until a smooth, wet dough is formed. Pour this mixture in with the flaxseed meal mixture. Stir until everything is well combined.

Oliverio

▶ Scrape the mixture onto a non-stick dehydrator sheet, spread to a little thicker than ¼ inch and dry for 1½ hours. Using a 2-inch cookie cutter, cut out 24 circles. Carefully transfer the circles to a mesh dehydrator sheet. Transfer the scraps to another mesh dehydrator sheet. Put both trays back into the dehydrator and continue drying for 12 hours for a crunchy-soft cookie. For a crisper cookie, continue drying for an additional 6 to 8 hours.

Make the mint cream

▶ In a high-speed or regular blender, combine the mint-cream ingredients and process until smooth. This will take a little time and you'll need to scrape down the sides of the blender. You will have little green bits of mint, but keep in mind that you won't see these because the cookies will be covered in chocolate.

▶ Put the mint cream in a bowl and set aside until ready to assemble the cookies.

▶ To assemble, divide the mint cream evenly among 12 cookies. Top with the remaining 12 cookies and gently press so that the cream comes all the way to the edges of the cookies. Put the cookies in the refrigerator for a few hours so that the cream firms up. This makes dipping the cookies in melted chocolate easier.

Dip the cookies

▶ In a double-boiler, carefully melt the chocolate chips. Remove from the heat and stir in the peppermint-flavored stevia and the coconut oil.

▶ Have a cooling rack at the ready. Working with one cookie at a time, dip it in the melted chocolate and using two forks, move the cookie through the chocolate until it is thoroughly coated. Put the cookie on one fork and gently tap it to remove excess chocolate. Then, drag the fork/cookie over the edge of the pot. Place the cookie on the rack and proceed with the remaining cookies. If you like, sprinkle the cookies with cacao nibs, or crumble up the cookie scraps and sprinkle them on top of the melted chocolate.

▶ Put the cookies in the refrigerator for 30 minutes to firm. Keep stored in the refrigerator.

Suggestions

▶ Skip the chocolate coating and make a chocolate sandwich cookie by omitting the mint leaves and peppermint stevia from the cream filling. Instead, add a teaspoon of vanilla-flavored stevia to the cream filling.

▶ For chocolate-orange cookies, omit the mint leaves and peppermint stevia and use a little orange zest and orange oil instead. Omit the peppermint from the chocolate coating.

Gluten-free ▲ Oil-free ▲ Easy
Prep time: **12–14 hours** *Cook time:* **20 minutes**

Chocolate

POPPY'S MEXICAN CHOCOLATE CAKE

serves 12 to 16

What would a chocolate chapter be without chocolate cake? Sad, that's what! Thankfully, my friend Poppy came to the rescue by creating this outstanding, rich cake that received rave reviews from my testers.

Cake
2 cups Gluten-Free All-Purpose Blend
    (see recipe on page 42) or your
    favorite gluten-free baking blend
1 cup ground almonds
2 heaping tsp. gluten-free baking powder
2 heaping tsp. baking soda
2 heaping Tbsp. cocoa or cacao powder
1/4 tsp. sea salt
2 tsp. ground cinnamon
Finely grated zest of 1/2 orange
2 cups cooked beetroot purée
1 cup Date Paste (see recipe on page 40)
1 cup pure maple syrup

1 cup puréed avocado
1/4 cup melted coconut oil
2 tsp. vanilla extract
1 cup chopped dark unsweetened
    chocolate (at least 70% cocoa),
    melted

Topping
1/2 cup canned light coconut milk
3/4 cup chopped dark unsweetened
    chocolate
1 tsp. vanilla extract
4 Tbsp. Date Paste
Dash cinnamon
Dash cayenne, optional

▶ Preheat oven to 325 degrees and line a 9-inch round cake pan.
▶ Whisk together the dry ingredients (flour through to zest) in a large mixing bowl.
▶ Mix the wet ingredients (beetroot through to melted chocolate) in a separate bowl, then add to the dry ingredients. Mix until fully combined.
▶ Bake for about 1 to 1½ hours or until a skewer inserted into the center comes out free of wet batter but with moist crumbs. Let cool for about 15 minutes before removing from the pan and placing on a wire rack.
▶ For the glaze, simply heat together the ingredients in a small pan over a medium heat, stirring to melt the chocolate and combine the ingredients. Let cool then pour over the cake to serve.

Gluten-free

PUMPKIN PIE SPICE CASHEW BUTTER CUPS

makes 20

I love a peanut butter cup as much as the next person, but sometimes a girl's gotta break out. Cashew butter has a superb creaminess and a natural sweetness. The spiced pumpkin purée brings a lovely color to the filling.

1 pound (about 3 cups) stevia-sweetened, semi-sweet chocolate
3/4 cup Cashew Butter (see recipe on page 53)
1/2 cup pumpkin purée

3/4 tsp. liquid stevia
1/2 tsp. ground cinnamon
1/4 tsp. ground ginger
1/4 tsp. ground cardamom
1/4 tsp. allspice

▶ Line 20 muffin cups with silicone (or paper) muffin liners. Divide the chocolate chips into two portions, setting aside ⅔ (about 2 cups) of the chips for later. In a double boiler, gently melt the other ⅓ (about 1 cup). With a large spoon, divide the melted chocolate between the 20 muffin cups, using the back of the spoon to spread the chocolate evenly over the bottoms of the cups. Put the muffin tins in the refrigerator to set the chocolate while you prepare the filling. No need to clean the double boiler as you'll be using it again.

▶ In a food processor, combine the cashew butter and remaining ingredients and process until smooth and creamy. Scrape the mixture into a bowl and if desired, chill for about 30 minutes to make it easier to work with when making the chocolate cups.

▶ Remove the muffin tins from the refrigerator and place dollops (about 2 teaspoons) of the cashew-pumpkin mixture on top of the chocolate. Using wet fingers or a wet offset spatula, spread the cashew-pumpkin mixture over the chocolate bottoms until it almost reaches the edge. You want a little chocolate to show so that the top layer of chocolate has something solid on which to adhere. Place the muffin tins back in the refrigerator.

▶ Remove and set aside ¼ cup of chips from the remaining ⅔ portion of chocolate chips. Melt the larger portion gently in a double boiler. Remove from the heat and stir in the reserved ¼ cup chocolate chips. Let sit for a few minutes and then stir until the chips have all melted. This is a cheater way to temper chocolate. Now, take the muffin tins out of the refrigerator once again and ladle chocolate on top of the cashew-pumpkin mixture, using the bottom of the spoon to spread and swirl the chocolate. Once all of the chocolate has been used up, put the muffin tins back in the refrigerator to set.

▶ Once set these chocolate cups are ready to eat! Keep them stored in the refrigerator. If you use silicone muffin cups, these babies pop right out.

Gluten-free
Total time: **40–60 minutes, excluding final chill time**

SARAH'S ALMOND & GOJI BERRY CHOCOLATE BARK

makes 16 pieces

This is one of Sarah's most popular recipes and with one bite into this rich treat, you'll understand why.

1 cup unrefined coconut oil
1 cup raw cacao powder
1/2 cup pure maple syrup, at room
    temperature
1 tsp. vanilla extract

2 Tbsp. raw almonds, roughly chopped
2 Tbsp. goji berries
2 Tbsp cacao nibs
1 tsp. large sea salt crystals

▶ Line an 8 × 8 pan with parchment paper allowing excess paper to hang over the sides.

▶ Melt the coconut oil over low heat.

▶ Combine the melted coconut oil, cacao powder, maple syrup, and vanilla extract in a small bowl and whisk together until completely smooth. Pour the chocolate into the prepared pan. Tap the pan gently on the counter to evenly distribute the chocolate and remove any air bubbles.

▶ Set the pan in the refrigerator for 10 minutes until it has firmed up just slightly. It should still be soft and sticky to the touch. Evenly sprinkle almonds, goji berries, cacao nibs, and sea salt over the top.

▶ Place the chocolate bark in the freezer for 15 minutes or until chocolate is frozen all the way through. Cut into sixteen 2 × 2–inch pieces. Store in an airtight container in the refrigerator for up to 5 days or freeze for longer storage.

Suggestions

▶ Maple syrup is not a raw food. Replace with ⅓ cup raw agave nectar to make a completely raw chocolate bark.

▶ If you like, stir in the almonds and goji berries with the other ingredients and sprinkle the cacao nibs on top of the bark after 10 minutes in the refrigerator. Gently press the nibs into the bark.

Gluten-free ▲ Raw option ▲ Quick ▲ Easy

Your mom's voice on the other end of the line.
Pillowy piles of soft white bubbles suspended on warm bath water.
The scent of lavender drifting on the summer breeze.
Watching the rain pour down from the sanctuary of your couch.
Snuggly, safe, soothing, soft.
Comfort.

craving 3
COMFORT

BAKED ALMOND BUTTER & APRICOT OATMEAL

serves 4

The origins of this recipe come from my month-long peanut butter and jelly blog posts in honor of Vegan Month of Food—a yearly blogging event where vegans from all over the world commit to sharing at least 20 vegan-centric recipes, articles, information, and commentary during the month of September. Based on feedback from my recipe testers, I made a few small but important changes to the original recipe.

1 cup uncooked gluten-free steel-cut oats
2 cups water
1/2 cup dried apricots, chopped into
    small pieces
1 Tbsp. fresh ginger, grated or minced
1/2 tsp. cinnamon
1/4 tsp. dried ginger

Pinch salt
1/3 cup smooth or chunky natural
    almond butter
Zest of 1/2 an orange
1/2 cup non-dairy milk
1/4 cup fresh orange juice
Slivered almonds for garnish, optional

▶ Combine the steel-cut oats and 2 cups water in a medium-sized saucepan and let sit for several hours or overnight.

▶ Place 4 ramekins on a small baking pan and preheat oven to 350 degrees. You can also use an 8 × 8 baking dish.

▶ Bring the oats/water to a boil, then reduce the heat to a simmer and cook until oats are tender, about 10 minutes. Add more water if the mixture becomes too dry. Stir in the ginger, apricots, cinnamon, almond butter, salt, and orange zest. When the almond butter is fully incorporated, remove the oats from the heat and stir in the milk and orange juice.

▶ Divide the oat mixture between the 4 ramekins or scrape into the baking dish and bake for 10 minutes. Sprinkle oatmeal with slivered almonds, if using.

Suggestions

▶ For extra fruitiness, top the oatmeal with spoonfuls of your favorite fruit-sweetened jam or jelly, or sprinkle on fresh berries.

Gluten-free ▲ Oil-free ▲ Easy

Prep time: **8–12 hours soaking** *Cook time:* **20 minutes**

CREAMY SCRAMBLED TOFU

serves 4

It took me a long time to even try tofu scrambles because I just couldn't imagine they could taste good. Now I love them and Kel and I enjoy a scramble at least once a week. What's great about tofu scrambles is the many ways they can be modified and adapted. I like to eat this extra-creamy version with a side of Tempeh Bacon, one of Kathy's Whole Wheat Veggie Quinoa Drop Biscuits, and a couple of roasted tomatoes sprinkled with fresh herbs.

1/3 cup cooked white beans
1/4 cup unsweetened Almond Milk (see
    recipe on page 35)
1 clove garlic
2 Tbsp. nutritional yeast
1 tsp. fresh lemon juice

Pinch turmeric
Pinch ground black pepper
Pinch kala namak, optional, or sea salt
14 ounces firm tofu, pressed for a few
    hours and drained
1/2 Tbsp. liquid aminos

▶ Put the white beans through the kala namak into a high-speed or regular blender and process until very smooth. Pour the mixture into a large bowl.

▶ Crumble the block of tofu into the bowl with the bean mixture and stir so that the tofu is completely coated.

▶ Add a splash of water or vegetable broth to a skillet and warm over medium-high heat. Add the tofu/bean mixture and sauté for 8 to 10 minutes, adding small splashes of water or broth as necessary so that the tofu doesn't stick to the pan. After about 10 minutes, let the water cook off, then add the liquid aminos. Stir to combine. Taste and adjust the seasonings.

▶ Divide the mixture between four plates and serve with your favorite breakfast fixin's.

Suggestions

▶ I've deliberately left this scramble fairly plain so that it can be dressed up as one wishes. Add sautéed mushrooms, bell peppers, and onions; or, stir in strips of corn tortillas while cooking the tofu and then serve with your favorite spicy salsa or a side of black beans.

Prep time: **3 hours, including time to press the tofu** *Cook time:* **10 minutes**

BEX'S EGGPLANT CHANA MASALA

serves 4 to 6

Nothing says comfort like a warming bowl of spicy Indian food—especially when you can get it onto the table and into tummies in under an hour.

1 large eggplant
1 tsp. sea salt
1 Tbsp. coconut oil, optional
2 small onions, finely chopped
2 cloves garlic, minced
2 tsp. grated fresh ginger
2 tsp. cumin
1/2 tsp. cayenne pepper
1 tsp. turmeric

2 tsp. paprika
1 tsp. garam masala
2 cups crushed tomatoes
1 cup water
3 cups cooked chickpeas (canned is fine, just rinse and drain)
Squeeze of lemon juice
1 cup fresh cilantro, chopped, divided

▶ Wash the eggplant, leaving the skin on and chop into 1-inch cubes. Discard the ends. Place cubes in a bowl and sprinkle with the 1 teaspoon sea salt.
▶ In a large saucepan over medium heat, sauté the onion in oil or in a splash of water or vegetable broth until translucent. Add garlic, ginger, and eggplant and cook, stirring often, for 10 minutes.
▶ Add the cumin, cayenne pepper, turmeric, paprika, and garam masala. Mix well to thoroughly coat the eggplant. Stir in the tomatoes, water, and chickpeas and simmer for 15 to 20 minutes.
▶ Remove the pan from the heat and stir in the lemon juice and half of the cilantro. Season with sea salt and pepper. Top with the remaining cilantro.

Suggestions
▶ Delicious served with brown basmati rice.

Gluten-free ▲ Easy
Total time: **45 minutes**

Comfort

DOLMADE-STUFFED BABY PEPPERS WITH LEMON-GARLIC CASHEW CREAM

makes 30 to 40

I love stuffed grape leaves—when someone else makes them. Unfortunately, they're usually heavy with olive oil and I prefer mine stuffed with brown rice rather than white. So, dolmade-stuffed peppers was born!

Peppers

Water or Vegetable Broth (see recipe on page 60) for sautéing
1 large onion, finely chopped
1 small fennel bulb, halved, cored, and finely chopped
2 cloves garlic, peeled and minced
Zest from 1 lemon
1/2 cup pine nuts
1 cup short-grain brown rice
2 cups Vegetable Broth, divided, or store-bought low-sodium broth
1/4 cup golden raisins
1/4 cup kalamata olives, chopped
1/4 cup fresh mint leaves, chopped

1 Tbsp. dried dill weed
Sea salt and ground black pepper, to taste
Juice of 2 lemons
30 to 40 small (snacking) bell peppers, tops cut and seeds/ribs removed.

Lemon-Garlic Cashew Cream

1/4 cup raw cashew pieces, soaked for a few hours, rinsed and drained
1/4 cup Vegetable Broth
2 Tbsp. fresh lemon juice
3-ounces silken tofu
1 clove garlic
1/2 tsp. nutritional yeast
pinch tsp. ground black pepper

▶ In a large sauce pan, sauté the onion, fennel, and garlic over medium heat in water or broth for about 10 minutes. Add the pine nuts and rice and stir, then add 1 cup vegetable broth. Simmer the rice for 20 to 30 minutes, or until most of the liquid has been absorbed. Put this mixture into a large bowl and stir in the raisins, olives, mint leaves, dill weed, salt and pepper. Set aside until cool.

▶ Preheat the oven to 375 degrees. When the rice mixture is cool enough to handle, fill each pepper with some filling, using a small spoon. Place the peppers tightly together in a large oven-safe casserole dish. Pour the remaining one cup of the vegetable broth along with the lemon juice into the casserole dish. The liquid should come nearly halfway up the peppers. Cover the dish and bake the peppers for about 1 hour, or until the peppers are very tender and the rice is cooked through.

▶ To make the sauce, put all of the ingredients in a high-speed or regular blender and process until very smooth—30 seconds to 1 minute. Pour into a small saucepan and warm gently over medium-low heat, stirring occasionally. The mixture will thicken as it warms, so you may need to add more vegetable broth or water.

▶ Serve the sauce alongside the stuffed peppers.

Suggestions
▶ Use about 6 large bell peppers in place of the baby bells.
▶ These would make a delicious appetizer for a party.

Gluten-free ▲ Oil-free
Cook time: **20–30 minutes** Prep time: **1 hour**

OATS E FAGIOLI

serves 4 to 6

Another simple yet hearty soup that is in regular rotation in my house.

1 large onion, diced
2 carrots, peeled and diced
2 stalks celery, diced
3 cloves garlic, minced
1 tsp. dried oregano
1/2 tsp. dried thyme
1/2 tsp. dried rosemary
1 cup oat groats*
1 Tbsp. liquid aminos or low-sodium tamari
1 Tbsp. tomato paste or Spicy Catsup

(see recipe on page 253)
1 (15-ounce) can petite-diced tomatoes
4 cups Vegetable Broth (see recipe on page 60) or store-bought low-sodium broth
2 (15-ounce) cans cannellini beans, rinsed and drained
4 cups spinach, roughly chopped
"Parmesan" Cheez, (see recipe on page 54) for topping, optional
Chopped fresh basil, for garnish, optional

▶ In a large pot, sauté the onions, carrots, celery, and garlic in a splash of water. Cook for about 5 minutes, or until the vegetables start to get tender. Stir in the spices and cook for another minute. Add the liquid aminos, tomato paste, tomatoes, the vegetable broth, and the beans.

▶ Bring to a boil, reduce the heat to a simmer, and cover the pot. Cook for about 20 minutes. Add the cooked oat groats and cook for an additional 30 minutes. Add water or vegetable broth if the soup becomes too thick.

▶ About five minutes before serving, stir in the spinach but don't cover the pot. When the spinach is limp but still bright green, the soup is ready to serve.

▶ While the soup is simmering, cook the oat groats. Put the groats in a small saucepan and cover with water. Bring to a boil, then reduce heat to a simmer—adding water as necessary. Cook for about 15 minutes. Add to the soup for the last 30 minutes of cooking.

▶ Top with "Parmesan" Cheez and/or fresh basil.

▶ Use any other white bean if you don't have cannellini beans.

▶ Use kale, beet greens, collard or mustard greens instead of the spinach; you may need to cook them a bit longer.

▶ Instead of oat groats, use a gluten-free pasta or regular pasta if you can digest wheat.

Gluten-free ▲ Oil-free ▲ Quick ▲ Easy

Prep time: **15 minutes** *Cook time:* **1 hour**

RATATOUILLE POLENTA CUPS
WITH MOM'S MARINARA SAUCE

makes 12

My dad went through a brief love affair with polenta and this dish is reminiscent of how he liked to prepare it. He baked his in a casserole pan and the filling was a big pile of spinach, sliced tomatoes, and mozzarella cheese. It was so simple and so good! Out of the oven the consistency was like pudding, but leftovers were sliceable.

For these, I suggest you make them ahead and reheat them so that the cute little muffin shape is retained, but of course you can serve it straight out of the oven. Just remember the cups will be extremely soft and fall apart.

Ratatouille
Water or Vegetable Broth for sautéing
    (see page 60 for recipe)
1/2 small onion, minced
1 clove garlic, minced
1 cup zucchini, finely chopped
1 cup eggplant, peeled and finely
    chopped
4 cremini or button mushrooms,
    stemmed and finely chopped (about
    1 cup)
1 large tomato, deseeded and finely
    chopped (about 1 cup)
1/2 tsp. dried oregano
1/2 tsp. dried thyme
1/4 tsp. dried rosemary

1/4 tsp. ground black pepper
Pinch sea salt
Polenta
4 cups Vegetable Broth
Pinch sea salt
1 1/4 cups polenta (the dry grain, not the
    pre-cooked kind in the tube)
2 Tbsp. "Parmesan Cheez" (see recipe on
    page 54) or nutritional yeast
1/2 tsp. dried thyme
1/4 tsp. ground black pepper
Dash red pepper flakes

Mom's Marinara Sauce (see recipe on
    page 49), for topping

▶ Place an ungreased 12-cup muffin tin onto a large baking sheet and set aside. Preheat the oven to 350 degrees.

▶ In a large skillet, heat the water or broth over medium-high heat and add the onion and garlic. Sauté for 2 to 3 minutes and add the zucchini, eggplant and mushrooms. Sauté for an additional 5 minutes. Add the tomato, spices, and sea salt and cook for another 1 to 2 minutes. Remove the pan from the heat and set aside until ready to assemble the polenta cups.

▶ In a medium-sized pot, bring the 4 cups water/broth and salt to a boil over medium-high heat. Stir in the polenta and whisk to break up any clumps. Turn down the heat to low and cover the pot. Cook the polenta for 12 to 15 minutes, adding water if it becomes too thick. Be sure to stir the polenta occasionally so that it doesn't stick to the bottom of the pot. The polenta should be tender, not crunchy, so keep adding water and cooking until it's soft.

▶ When the polenta is tender, stir in the "Parmesan" Cheez or nutritional yeast, thyme, and black pepper, and red pepper flakes. Taste and adjust the seasonings. Using a spoon, ladle about one heaping tablespoon of polenta into the bottom of each muffin tin and spread it to completely cover the bottom. Divide the ratatouille mixture between the 12 cups and then divide the remainder of the polenta on top of the ratatouille, spreading it down into the cups so that the filling is covered.

▶ Place the baking sheet with the muffin tins into the oven and bake for about 30 minutes, or until the top of the polenta has browned in spots and the filling is bubbling.

▶ Let cool and then store the muffin tin, covered, in the refrigerator. When ready to serve, run a knife around the polenta cups, lift out, and gently warm them in the microwave. Top with Mom's Marinara Sauce.

Suggestions
▶ To make things really easy, stir the ratatouille into the polenta and then ladle everything into a deep 9 × 9 baking pan.

Gluten-free ▲ Oil-free ▲ Easy

RED LENTIL & VEGETABLE CURRY SOUP

serves 4 to 6

1 large onion, chopped
2 cups chopped cauliflower
1 large sweet potato, peeled and
    chopped into 1/2-inch cubes
2 cloves garlic, minced
1/2 tsp. brown or black mustard seeds
1 tsp. ground ginger
1 1/2 tsp. curry powder
Pinch red pepper flakes, optional
1 1/2 cups red lentils, sorted through and
    rinsed

4 cups Vegetable Broth (see recipe on
    page 60) or store-bought low-
    sodium broth
Juice of 1/2 a lemon (about 1 Tbsp.)
1 tsp. pure maple syrup
1 (15-ounce) can light coconut milk
4 cups spinach, roughly chopped
Chopped cilantro, for garnish

▶ In a large pot, water sauté the onions, cauliflower, sweet potato, and garlic for 8 to 10 minutes over medium-high heat, adding more water as needed to keep the vegetables from sticking or burning.
▶ Stir in the mustard seeds, ground ginger, curry powder, red pepper flakes, if using, and red lentils and cook for an additional 1 to 2 minutes. Add the vegetable broth, lemon juice, and maple syrup and bring the soup to a boil. Lower the heat to a simmer, cover the pot, and cook the soup for 20 minutes, stirring occasionally.
▶ Add the coconut milk and chopped spinach, stir, and cook the soup until the spinach is wilted, but still bright green. Serve the soup with chopped cilantro.

Suggestions
▶ Load up this soup with your favorite vegetables.

Gluten-free ▲ Oil-free ▲ Quick ▲ Easy
Prep time: **10 minutes** *Cook time:* **30 minutes**

Comfort

SOUTHWESTERN POT PIE

serves 4 to 6

Pot pies are one of my favorite cold-weather comfort dishes. They are a bit labor intensive, but sometimes it's well worth spending a little time in the kitchen. When it's frosty cold outside, there isn't really a better place to be anyway.

Crust

3/4 cup whole wheat pastry flour or
    Gluten-Free All-Purpose Flour Blend
    (see recipe on page 42)
1 Tbsp. nutritional yeast
1 Tbsp. flaxseed meal
1/4 tsp. garlic powder
1/4 tsp. dried onion flakes
1/4 tsp. ground black pepper
1/4 tsp. chile powder
Pinch cumin
Pinch sea salt
6 Tbsp. tahini
1/4 tsp. pure maple syrup
3 to 5 Tbsp. ice water

Filling

Water or vegetable broth for sautéing
1 medium onion, diced
1 medium red bell pepper, cored,
    seeded, and diced
3 cloves garlic, minced
2 tsp. chile powder
1 tsp. garlic powder
1 tsp. dried onion flakes
1 tsp. cumin
1/2 tsp. ground black pepper
Pinch sea salt
2 medium tomatoes, cored, seeded, and
    chopped
1 (4-ounce) can mild (or hot) diced green
    chiles
1 (15-ounce) can black beans, rinsed and
    drained
2 Red Hots Hot Dogs (see recipe on page
    250–1) or 2 store-bought, vegan
    chipotle sausages, sliced into 1/4-
    inch rounds
1 cup Vegetable Broth (see recipe on
    page 60) or store-bought low-
    sodium broth
2 Tbsp. arrowroot powder
1/2 cup fresh cilantro, chopped
Tofu & Cashew Sour Cream (see recipe
    on page 61), for garnish, if desired
Chipotle Salsa (see recipe on page 245)
    or store-bought salsa for garnish, if
    desired

▶ Put the flour, nutritional yeast, flaxseed meal, garlic powder, dried onion flakes, black pepper, chile powder, cumin, and sea salt in the bowl of a food processor. Pulse a few times to combine. Add the tahini and maple syrup and pulse a few times to incorporate.

▶ With the motor running, slowly pour in the ice water until a dough ball forms. Remove the dough from the bowl and knead a few times to create a smooth, uniform ball. Flatten into a small disk, cover with plastic wrap and place in the refrigerator until ready to use.

▶ Heat a large skillet over medium-high heat, add a splash of water or broth. Sauté the onion, bell pepper, and garlic for 8 to 10 minutes, or until soft. Stir in the spices and salt and cook for an additional minute. Add the tomatoes, green chiles, black beans, and hot dogs or sausage slices. Cook for about 5 minutes.

▶ Whisk together the 1 cup vegetable broth and the arrowroot powder and then pour this into the bean mixture. Let the mixture come to a boil and then remove the pan from the heat once the liquid has thickened. Stir in the cilantro.

▶ Preheat the oven to 350 degrees. Pour the bean mixture into an 8 × 8 baking dish and set aside.

▶ On a lightly floured surface, roll the dough into a roughly 8 × 8 square (or circle—whatever is easiest) and then cut into 4 equal pieces. Lay the dough pieces on top of the filling in the baking dish. Bake the pot pie for 40 to 45 minutes, or until the filling is bubbly and the crust is dry and crumbly. Let the pot pie rest for about 10 minutes before serving.

▶ Divide the pot pie between four shallow bowls and top with vegan sour cream and salsa, if desired.

Suggestions
▶ If you don't like or don't have vegan sausages, add chopped, cooked potato or a cup of corn.

Gluten-free Option ▲ Oil-free
Total time: **1 hour 15 minutes**

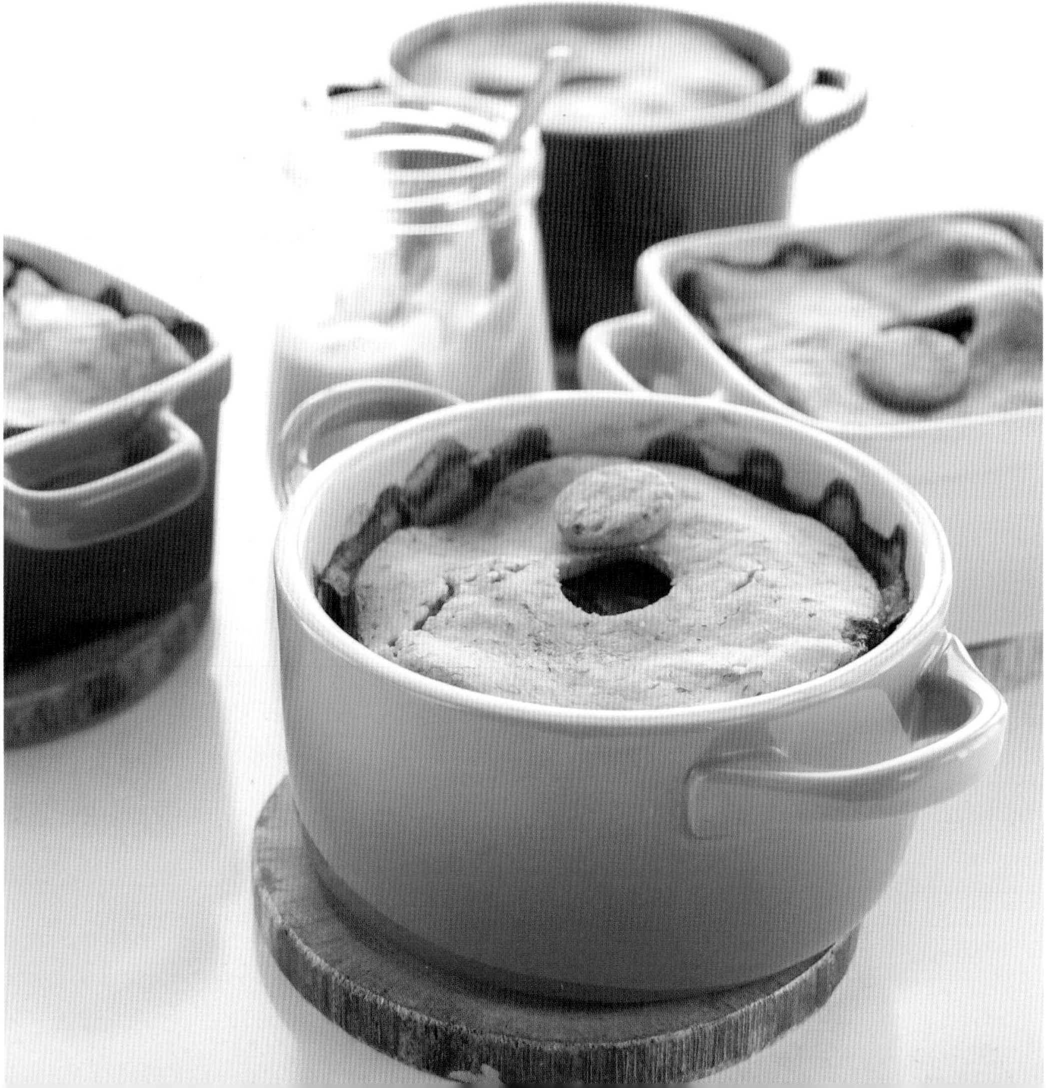

TERESA'S BLACK SOYBEANS WITH CHESTNUTS & SHIITAKE MUSHROOMS

serves 4

Teresa is a whiz at creating simple meals that are full of flavor but also pack a powerful nutritional punch. This stew is pure comfort food.

Barley malt powder is made by toasting sprouted barley and then pulverizing it. Barley malt syrup is also made with sprouted barley, using the grain's own enzymes created during the sprouting process. With about half of the sweetness of refined sugar, barley malt doesn't cause the high spikes in glucose associated with consuming the white stuff. You can use both the powdered form of barley malt and the thick syrup in baked goods, as I do when I make bagels, to give them that authentic New York deli-style flavor.

1/3 cup dried chestnuts, soaked for 8 hours or overnight
4 to 5 medium dried shiitake mushrooms, soaked for 20 minutes
1 1/2 cups black soybeans, sorted, rinsed and soaked for 8 hours or overnight
2-inch piece of dried kombu or kelp
a few pinches sea salt
1/2 tsp. shoyu or tamari
2 tsp. barley malt syrup or to taste

▶ Drain the chestnuts. Using a chopstick, remove any bits of shell that are stuck in the cracks of the chestnuts.

▶ Drain the mushrooms and save the soaking water to add to the cooking liquid. Cut any hard stems off the mushrooms and discard. Cut each mushroom into 2 to 4 slices.

▶ Drain the soybeans and place in small or medium-sized pressure cooker. Pour in fresh water to cover by a little less than 1 inch. Add the mushroom soaking liquid. Bring to a boil on medium heat and scrape off any foam that rises to the surface. Add the chestnuts, mushrooms and kombu. Place lid on and bring to pressure. Reduce heat to the lowest you can while still maintaining pressure. Cook for 50 minutes. Remove from heat and let pressure come down naturally.

▶ Remove lid. Place pot on low heat. Add a few pinches sea salt and the shoyu or tamari and let simmer gently for about 10 minutes. Remove from heat and add the barley malt. Stir well, but gently, to combine, trying to keep the chestnuts from breaking up too much.

Gluten-free ▲ Oil-free ▲ Easy

Total time: **10 hours, including soaking time**

VEGETABLE FRIED QUINOA & BROWN RICE

serves 4

It was a revelation to me when I realized one of my favorite restaurant dishes could be made without oil. This is one of those meals that I turn to often—not only for its ease and versatility—but because I find it extremely comforting and homey. Next time you cook up some quinoa or brown rice, make extra so that you can quickly put together this delicious stir-fry.

Vegetable Broth (see page 60 for recipe), for sautéing
1 onion, chopped
1 red bell pepper, cored and chopped
1 carrot, peeled in thinly sliced
8 ounces cremini or button mushrooms, stemmed and thinly sliced
1 cup shelled edamame (thawed if frozen)
1 cup snow peas, ends and strings removed
2 cloves garlic, minced

1 tsp. fresh ginger, grated or finely minced
1/4 cup mirin
1/4 cup low-sodium tamari or soy sauce
1/2 tsp. garlic chili paste, or to taste
3 cups cooked short grain brown rice
1 cup cooked red or white quinoa
Ground black pepper, to taste
Chopped cilantro, for garnish
Roasted peanuts, for garnish
Limes, quartered
Hot sauce

▶ Have all of the ingredients ready to go before you heat up a wok or large skillet. Once fried rice gets going, you won't have time for chopping or measuring!

▶ Heat a wok or large skillet to medium-high. Splash in some vegetable broth or water and sauté the onions, bell pepper, and carrot for about 4 minutes. Remove from the pan and set aside. Add another splash of broth and add the mushrooms, edamame, and snow peas. Sauté for about 4 minutes. Remove from the pan and set aside.

▶ Add another splash of vegetable broth and sauté the garlic and ginger for 30 seconds. Add the rice and quinoa, stirring, until the broth cooks off. Pour in the mirin and stir until it has cooked off.

▶ Put all of the vegetables back into the pan, sprinkle with ground black pepper, and stir to combine. Add the tamari or soy sauce and garlic chile paste, stir a few times and then remove the pan from the heat.

▶ Divide the fried rice between four big bowls and top with cilantro and peanuts; squirt each portion with lime and be sure to have the hot sauce for those who like their fried rice spicy.

Suggestions

▶ Use your favorite vegetables in place of those listed here.

▶ Add chopped pineapple towards the end of the cooking time.

▶ Add cubes of marinated baked tofu.

Gluten-free ▲ Oil-free ▲ Quick ▲ Easy

Prep time: **15 minutes** *Cook time:* **20 minutes**

Steve McQueen in Bullitt.
A 1965 Shelby GT 350 Mustang.
Crushed mint leaves.
An icy drop of water sliding down the back of your neck.
Cannonballing into the old swimming hole.
Refreshing, invigorating, reviving, frosty.
Cool.

craving 4
COOL

BUTTER LETTUCE WEDGES WITH SUNFLOWER SEED DRESSING, PEARS, & TEMPEH BACON

serves 4

This take on a classic salad reminds me of many family dinners eaten out at The Brown Derby: a big, crunchy wedge of lettuce topped with a creamy dressing and sprinkled with salty bacon. My version subs tempeh for bacon and adds a little sweetness with fresh pears.

Dressing
1/2 cup raw sunflower seeds
1/2 cup non-dairy milk
1/4 cup apple cider vinegar
1 clove garlic
1 tsp. Dijon mustard
1/4 tsp. ground black pepper
Pinch sea salt
1 tsp. dried chives, or 1 Tbsp. fresh chives, chopped

1 Tbsp. fresh parsley, chopped

Salad
2 large heads butter lettuce, cut into quarters
2 ripe pears, cored and thinly sliced
1 recipe Tempeh Bacon (see recipe on page 63), crumbled or chopped (exclude if going for 100% raw)

▶ Add the sunflower seeds through the salt in a high-speed or regular blender and process until very smooth. Add the chives and parsley and pulse a few times to incorporate. Set aside.

▶ Place two butter lettuce wedges each in four bowls. Divide the pear slices, the tempeh bacon and the dressing between the bowls. Serve.

Suggestions
▶ If the dressing is too thick, add water, a little bit at at time, to get the consistency you like.

Gluten-free ▲ Raw option ▲ Oil-free ▲ Quick ▲ Easy
Total time: **15 minutes**

HIBISCUS-CHERRY COOLER

serves 2 to 3

More than just a pretty flower, hibiscus, when dried, becomes a tart and tangy tea. Drinking it regularly could lower blood pressure and some studies have shown that consuming the tea might help fight cancer—in particular brain and skin cancer.

A couple of cautions: if you have low blood pressure, you may want to limit your intake of hibiscus tea. Also, this tea can lower estrogen levels—if you're on hormone replacement therapy or are on birth control pills, this tea is not for you. It is also contraindicated during pregnancy. If you are undergoing chemotherapy—check with your physician before making this tea a regular part of your day.

1 1/2 cups hibiscus tea, chilled
2 oranges, peeled, or about 1/2 cup
    orange juice
1 lime, peeled

2 ripe bananas
2 to 4 Medjool dates, pitted and chopped
2 cups frozen cherries
1 Tbsp. hemp protein powder, optional

▶ Put all ingredients in a high-speed or regular blender and process until very smooth.

Substitutions
▶ Try using strawberries in place of the cherries.

Gluten-free ▲ High raw ▲ Oil-free ▲ Quick ▲ Easy
Total time: **5 minutes**

Cool

139

MANGO, PINEAPPLE, & CUCUMBER SMOOTHIE

serves 4

If you haven't guessed already, fruits and vegetables are loaded with antioxidants—the powerful compounds that keep free radicals at bay and help our bodies to defend themselves against cancer. When you can get it, add fresh (or frozen) mango to your diet. It's deliciously sweet, of course, and lends creaminess to smoothies—but it also contains fiber, plus a good dose of vitamins C and A to boost the immune system and benefit health.

1 cup coconut water or water
1 1/2 cups fresh pineapple, cut into chunks
1 large apple, peeled if not organic, cored, and cut into chunks
1 large mango, peeled, pitted and cut into chunks

1 large banana, cut into chunks
1/2 cup cucumber, peeled, seeded, and chopped
2 cups packed spinach and/or kale
1 tsp. fresh ginger, grated or minced

▶ Place all ingredients in a high-speed or regular blender and process until smooth. Divide among four glasses and serve.

Suggestions
▶ Use 1 to 1½ cups frozen pineapple and mango instead of fresh, though you may need additional water.
▶ Use peaches instead of mango.
▶ For an even creamier, richer smoothie, use your favorite non-dairy milk instead of water.

Gluten-free ▲ Raw ▲ Oil-free ▲ Quick ▲ Easy
Total time: **5 minutes**

RAW TOMATO–TOMATO SOUP FOR TWO

serves 2

I go with cherry tomatoes here because even off-season it's possible to get sweet and flavorful fruits. However, if you have home-grown or farmer's market tomatoes, definitely use those!

3 cups cherry tomatoes
2 to 3 very ripe strawberries
1 Tbsp. chopped sun-dried tomatoes
    (not in oil), soaked in warm water for
    about 15 minutes, drained
1 tsp. white miso paste

1/2 tsp. fresh lemon juice
1 small clove garlic, optional
Pinch ground black pepper and sea salt
Dash cayenne, optional
Fresh basil, for garnish, if desired

▶ Place all ingredients in a blender and process until smooth. Divide the soup between two small bowls, sprinkle with chopped basil and serve.

Suggestions
▶ For richness, add 2 teaspoons of almond paste in with the other ingredients and blend.

Gluten-free ▲ Raw ▲ Quick ▲ Easy
Total time: **10 minutes**

Cool

ROASTED APRICOT & COCONUT POPSICLES

serves 6

I've tried and tried to love fresh apricots—but still prefer them dried or baked, preferably in a tart or crumble. Going for something different, I roasted fresh apricots to maximize their sweetness. You might be tempted to eat this mixture straight out of the blender but be strong and make popsicles instead!

8 fresh apricots, pitted and chopped
1/2 cup full-fat coconut milk
2 Tbsp. plain coconut yogurt

1 Tbsp. pure maple syrup
1/4 to 1/2 tsp. coconut extract

▶ Preheat the oven to 375 degrees and bake the apricots in a small baking dish for 25 to 30 minutes. The apricots will be very soft and will have released a lot of their juice. Let the apricots cool completely before proceeding with the recipe.
▶ Put the apricots with all of their juice (and skins) along with the other ingredients in a blender and process until very smooth.
▶ Divide the mixture between 6 popsicle molds (each mold holding about 4 ounces each). You want to leave about ¼ inch of room at the top of the mold because the mixture will expand as it freezes. Freeze for about 6 hours or until solid. To remove the popsicles from the mold, run the molds briefly under warm water.

Suggestions
▶ The number of popsicles you get will depend on the size of your molds. I use molds that hold about 4 ounces each. Follow your particular mold's directions for filling and freezing.

Gluten-free ▲ Oil-free ▲ Easy
Total time: **5 minutes**

SUNSHINE SMOOTHIE

serves 2

The happy, bright color of this smoothie makes any morning feel as if its full of sunshine. But its beauty is more than skin-deep. This smoothie is packed with cancer-fighting properties—from inhibiting cancer cell growth to wiping out existing cancer cells—so be sure to drink up every last drop! If you are undergoing cancer treatment combined with nutrition therapy that calls for lessening or eliminating the consumption of fruit, skip this smoothie.

1 cup water
2 oranges, peeled (leave a little bit of peel)
1 large grapefruit, peeled (leave a little bit of peel)
1 ripe banana

1 mango, pitted and peeled
1-inch piece of ginger, peeled
1/2 cup chopped carrots
2-inch piece of fresh turmeric, peeled
2 Medjool dates, optional

▶ Add all ingredients to a high-speed or regular blender and process until very smooth. Serve immediately.

Suggestions
▶ Throw in a few mint leaves.
▶ Handle fresh turmeric root with care—it stains!

Gluten-free ▲ Oil-free ▲ Raw ▲ Quick ▲ Easy
Total time: **5 minutes**

SWEET POTATO PIE & APPLE PIE ICE CREAM IN MINI CRUSTS

serves 4

This is what happens when something hot (roasted sweet tater) meets something cool and creamy.

Ice Cream
2 ripe bananas, cut into chunks and frozen
1 sweet apple, such as Honeycrisp,
    cored, cut into chunks and frozen
1 1/2 cups roasted sweet potato, cut into
    chunks and frozen
5 Medjool dates, chopped, soaked in water
    for about 15 minutes, and drained
1 cup non-dairy milk (I prefer soy milk here)

2 Tbsp. tahini
1 tsp. vanilla extract
1 1/2 tsp. cinnamon
1/4 tsp. cardamom
1/4 tsp. ginger
Pinch allspice
1 batch Gluten-Free Sweet Pie Dough or
    Whole Wheat Sweet Pie Dough (see
    recipe on pages 56–58)

▶ Make the mini-crusts first. Preheat the oven to 425 degrees and set aside an 8- or 12-muffin tin. (No need to oil them.) Line a small baking sheet with parchment and set aside.

▶ Prepare the pie dough as directed. Remove the dough from the bowl of the processor and knead until a smooth ball forms. Flatten it slightly and place it on a lightly floured surface. Sprinkle more flour on top of the dough and roll it out until it's about ¼-inch thick. Using a 3½-inch round cookie cutter, cut out eight circles and gently press them into the muffin tin. Gather the dough scraps, knead, and roll out again. This time, use smaller round cookie cutters to make circles. You'll use these as garnish. Place these onto the small baking sheet.

▶ Bake the dough cups and the dough circles for about 12 minutes. Check them often to make sure they aren't burning; they'll go from perfect to burnt in the blink of an eye. Remove from the oven and let cool completely.

▶ For the ice cream, combine all of the ice cream ingredients in a high-speed blender and process until very smooth and creamy. You'll need to tamp the mixture several times to get it smooth. Scrape the mixture into an ice cream machine and follow the manufacturer's directions for freezing (mine takes about 25 minutes to reach the right consistency). Scoop ice cream into pie cups and garnish with pastry rounds and serve immediately, or store in an air-tight container in the freezer. (If frozen, let the ice cream sit at room temperature for a while to soften before serving.) Individually wrap the pie crusts and store in the freezer.

Gluten-free option ▲ Oil-free

Prep time: 12 hours, including freezing

Cook time: 30–40 minutes, including time in ice cream machine

WATERMELON COOLER

serves 2

Four ingredients. Perfect, thirst-quenching summer refreshMINT.

4 cups chilled watermelon, roughly
    chopped
1 cup red or green grapes, chilled or
    frozen

1/4 cup tightly-packed fresh mint leaves
1 tsp. fresh lemon juice

— —

▶ Place ingredients in a blender and process until smooth. Serve.

Gluten-free ▲ Oil-free ▲ Raw ▲ Quick ▲ Easy

Swirls of cold soft-serve piled high on a cake cone.
A white mountain of whipped coconut cream balanced
precariously atop a sea of hot chocolate.
Billowing towers of white clouds as seen from A9 at 30,000 feet.
Fluffy, feathery, lush, dreamy.
Creamy.

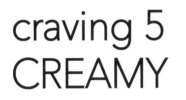

craving 5
CREAMY

ALMOND-COCONUT MILK

makes 5 cups

2 cups raw almonds, soaked 8 to 12 hours, rinsed and drained
1 cup unsweetened coconut flakes,

soaked for 15 minutes and drained
4 1/2 to 5 cups filtered water
2 Tbsp. Date Paste (see page 40 for recipe)

▷ Place almonds, coconut flakes, and water in a high-speed blender and process for about 1 minute. Check the consistency. Add more water if your prefer a thinner milk.

▷ Place a nut bag or fine-mesh colander over a large bowl or large measuring cup. Pour the almond-coconut mixture into the bag/colander. If using a nut bag, squeeze it to extract as much milk out of it as you can.

▷ Pour the milk back into a clean blender and add the date paste. Blend for about 30 seconds.

▷ Store milk in the refrigerator for up to 5 days. Reserve the pulp to use in baked goods, crackers, or in the "Parmesan" Cheez recipe on page 54.

Suggestions

▷ Use your favorite nut instead of almonds.

▷ Add 1 teaspoon of vanilla extract.

Gluten-free ▲ Oil-free ▲ Raw ▲ Quick ▲ Easy
Total time: **12 hours (soaking time) and 10 minutes**

Creamy

CARROT CAKE PUDDING

serves 6

I've recently discovered kuzu root powder and have been experimenting with it in sauces—and as here—in puddings. Kuzu contains no fat, is low in calories, and has virtually no taste. It is used not only a thickening agent, but also is used to treat stomach and digestion issues, to stimulate appetite, as an aid to relieve diarrhea and even as a cold remedy. And you thought this was just going to be a bowl of pudding!

2 cups fresh or bottled carrot juice (make sure it's 100% carrot juice)
2 cups coconut milk
2 Tbsp. pure maple syrup
1 tsp. ground cinnamon
1/2 tsp. ground ginger

1/8 tsp. ground cloves
1/8 tsp. cardamom
5 Tbsp. kuzu root powder
Whipped Coconut Cream (see recipe on page 64), for topping, optional
Golden raisins, for garnish, optional

▶ Combine all ingredients in a bowl or a large measuring cup. Remove ½ cup of the liquid and pour the remainder of the mixture into a small saucepan. Whisk together the ½ cup of the mixture and 5 tablespoons kuzu root powder and stir until completely dissolved. Set aside.

▶ Bring the mixture in the saucepan to a boil and whisk in the reserved liquid. Whisk constantly until the pudding begins to thicken. Remove from the heat and let sit for a few minutes while you get 6 glasses or bowls. Divide the liquid between the glasses and place them in the refrigerator to set, 4 to 6 hours.

Suggestions
▶ Whisk the mixture thoroughly as kuzu clumps easily.

Gluten-free ▲ Oil-free ▲ Easy
Cook time: **15 minutes** *Set time:* **4–6 hours**

EMBARRASINGLY SIMPLE BANANA BOWL

serves 2

This recipe goes back a long ways. When I was a bottomless-stomach of a kid and I'd whine to my mom about being hungry, she'd suggest I eat what her mom gave her as a bottomless-stomach kind of kid growing up in the late 30s and early 40s: slice a banana, add heavy cream, and sprinkle liberally with sugar. I've modified it to fit in with the way that I eat today, but the result is just as satisfying, delicious, and comforting as the original. Do try to use homemade nut milk here—and the Malted Milk (see recipe on page 160) is especially good for this. The creamy richness goes perfectly with the sweet bananas.

2 large bananas, sliced on the bias
"Malted" Milk (the amount depends on how much you want to use)
Chopped pecans or walnuts

▶ Divide the banana slices between two small bowls. Pour on the "Malted" Nut Milk and sprinkle with chopped nuts. Fill your bottomless stomach.

Suggestions
▶ Get fancy and add some fresh berries.
▶ Need some additional crunch? Top with lightly-sweetened whole-grain or gluten-free cereal or with the High Raw Blueberry Granola on page 178.

Gluten-free ▲ Raw ▲ Oil-free ▲ Quick ▲ Easy
Total time: 5 minutes tops

Creamy

"MALTED" MILK

makes 4 cups

Malt is made when barley or other grains have been germinated and dried with hot air, a process that converts starches into sugars. There's no malt in this rich nut milk, but the maca powder does an excellent job of mimicking malt's unique flavor—while adding fiber, calcium, magnesium, iron, vitamin C, and a wide range of B vitamins.

4 cups Almond or Almond-Coconut Milk
    (see recipe on page 35 or page 153)
3 Tbsp. Date Paste (see recipe on page 40)

2 1/2 Tbsp. maca powder
1 1/2 tsp. vanilla extract

▶ Place all ingredients in a blender and process until thoroughly combined. Store in the refrigerator for up to 5 days.

Gluten-free ▲ Raw ▲ Oil-free ▲ Quick ▲ Easy
Total time: **5 minutes**

PECAN PIE PUDDING

serves 4

This rich and creamy dessert gets its pie flavor from pecans, of course, but also from vanilla, malty maca powder, and smoky maple syrup.

Crust
1/2 cup chopped pecans
1/2 cup gluten-free rolled oats
1/4 cup puffed quinoa, optional
1/2 tsp. ground cinnamon
2 Tbsp. pure maple syrup
1 tsp. vanilla extract

Pudding
1 cup raw cashew pieces, soaked for a
    few hours, rinsed and drained

1/4 cup raw pecans, soaked with the
    cashews, rinsed and drained
6 Medjool dates, pitted and soaked with
    the cashews, rinsed and drained
1 (13.6-ounce) can light coconut milk
1 Tbsp. maca powder
2 tsp. vanilla extract

▶ Make the crust first by heating a non-stick skillet over medium-low heat. Add the pecans, oats, and puffed quinoa, if using, and lightly toast. This should take about 5 minutes. Watch closely and stir often. Remove pan from the heat. In a small bowl, whisk together the cinnamon, maple syrup, and vanilla extract. Stir in the pecan mixture, making sure everything is well-combined. Place approximately two tablespoons of the mixture in each of four glasses or bowls. Set aside the remainder of the pecan mixture.

▶ In a high-speed or regular blender, combine all of the pudding ingredients and process until silky-smooth. Divide the mixture between the four glasses or bowls. Top with the remaining crust—about two tablespoons per serving. Chill until firm.

Suggestions
▶ Serve with Whipped Coconut Cream (recipe on page 64), if desired.

Gluten-free ▲ High raw ▲ Oil-free ▲ Quick ▲ Easy
Total time: **10 minutes**

Creamy

ROASTED GARLIC & FRESH HERB CREAM CHEEZ

A.K.A. VEGAN BOURSIN

makes 2 small rounds

Diana, blogger at VeggieNextDoor.com, and one of my recipe testers, warns that this might not be the best snack for a party setting since one is guaranteed to have garlic-breath. But what's a little dragon breath among friends?!

1 small head garlic
4 Tbsp. fresh chopped herbs, such as thyme, rosemary, chives, and/or oregano
1 cup raw cashew pieces, soaked in water 8 to 10 hours, rinsed and drained

1/4 cup Coconut Butter (see recipe on page 37) or 1/4 cup unsweetened coconut flakes, soaked in water for about 15 minutes, drained
1/4 tsp. sea salt
1/2 to 1 tsp. garlic powder
3 Tbsp. fresh lemon juice

▶ Preheat toaster oven (or oven) to 450 degrees. Cut off the top third or so of the garlic and wrap the head in foil. Place the garlic in the oven and roast for 30 to 45 minutes, or until fragrant and very soft. Remove from the oven and allow to cool completely before unwrapping.

▶ Line two ¾ cup ramekins with cheesecloth. Sprinkle the bottoms of the ramekins with one tablespoon each of the herbs, reserving the remaining herbs.

▶ Meanwhile, in a food processor, process the cashew pieces, coconut butter or coconut flakes, and salt until fairly smooth. (It will not get completely smooth.) Squeeze the cloves from the roasted garlic and drop into the bowl of the food processor. Add the garlic powder and the lemon juice and process until thoroughly combined.

▶ Divide the mixture between the prepared ramekins, pressing the cheese down into the herbs and cheesecloth. Tap the ramekins on the counter a few times and level the top. Divide the remaining herbs between the two ramekins, gently press them into the cheese and cover with the ends of the cheesecloth. Put one ramekin on top of the other and fill a third ramekin with water and place it on top of both ramekins (you'll have a "tower" of 3 ramekins). Place them in the refrigerator and let set overnight.

Oliverio

▶ The next day, remove the water-filled ramekin. Gently tug the cheesecloth to remove the cream cheese from the other ramekins and serve with bread or crackers—or place them in an air-tight container for up to one week.

Suggestions
▶ If you use the Coconut Butter rather than the coconut flakes, you may need to add just a touch of water when processing.
▶ I give a range of garlic powder here because it's pretty powerful stuff. As the cheese sets, the flavor develops, so err on the side of less garlic powder (or none) if you're not a big fan.

Gluten-free ▲ High raw ▲ Quick ▲ Easy
Total time: **48 hours, including soaking, roasting, and setting time**

TRAVELIN' OATS

serves 2 to 3

For additional flavor, Maggie, a trusty recipe tester and blogger at CookbookAficionado.com, suggests toasting the coconut before adding it to the oats.

1 cup gluten-free rolled oats
2 cups unsweetened coconut milk (the kind in the carton or box)
1/4 cup unsweetened coconut flakes
1/4 cup dried blueberries or cranberries
1 heaping Tbsp. Date Paste (see recipe on page 40) or 2 Tbsp. pure maple syrup

1 tsp. vanilla extract
1 Tbsp. chia seeds
1 Tbsp. hemp seeds
1 tsp. cinnamon
1 tsp. fresh grated ginger root

▶ In a medium-sized bowl, combine all of the ingredients and stir thoroughly. Divide between two or three pint-sized mason jars. Store in the refrigerator or cooler (if traveling) for 8 plus hours. Serve with additional coconut or non-dairy milk.

Suggestions
▶ Substitute ½ cup of buckwheat groats for ½ cup of the rolled oats.

Gluten-free ▲ Raw ▲ Oil-free ▲ Quick ▲ Easy
Total time: **8 minutes**

Breaking through the brittle ice and into the deep, soft snow.
Digging into the box of popcorn in a darkened theater as the movie begins.
Your friend in Boulder, still wearing Birkenstocks and tie-dye.
Crisp, crackly, crumbly, crusty.
Crunchy.

craving 6
CRUNCHY

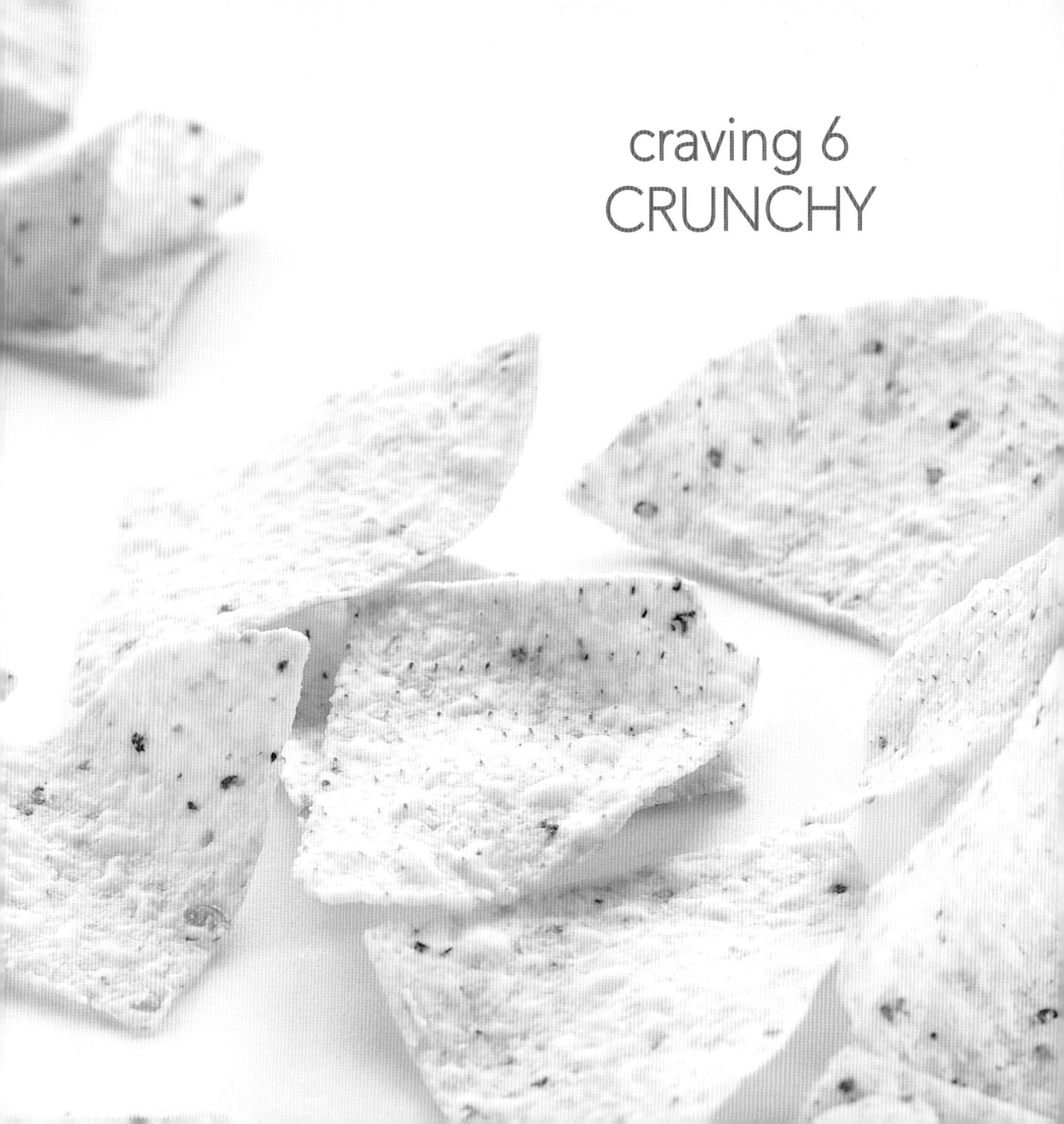

APPLE-CELERY-RICE SALAD
WITH PARSLEY-WALNUT DRESSING

serves 4

This refreshing and different salad is cool, crunchy, tart, and sweet.

Dressing
1/2 cup walnuts, soaked for 1 to 2 hours, rinsed and drained
1 cup loosely-packed fresh parsley
1/2 cup non-dairy milk
2 Tbsp. apple cider vinegar
2 tsp. fresh lemon juice
1/2 tsp. dried thyme
1 small clove garlic
Pinch sea salt and ground black pepper

Salad
1 medium-sized tart apple, such as Granny Smith, cored and cut into bite-sized chunks
1 medium-sized sweet apple, such as Fuji or Gala, cored and cut into bite-sized chunks
2 stalks celery, chopped (about 1/2 cup)
1 1/4 cups cooked brown rice
3 to 4 green onions, chopped
1/4 cup walnuts, roughly chopped
Sea salt and ground black pepper, to taste

▶ Place all of the dressing ingredients in a high-speed or regular blender and process until smooth.
▶ In a large bowl, toss together the apples, celery, rice, green onions, and walnuts. Pour the dressing over top and stir to thoroughly coat the salad. Chill for a couple of hours.
▶ To serve, top with additional chopped walnuts and parsley, if desired.

Suggestions
▶ Use any non-dairy milk that you like, but I find that the strong taste of soy milk overpowers the dressing.
▶ Feel free to use another cooked grain in place of the brown rice.

Gluten-free ▲ High raw ▲ Oil-free ▲ Quick ▲ Easy

KRISTY'S MAPLE-GLAZED
CINNAMON ROASTED CHICKPEAS

serves 4 to 5

Crunchy and sweet with the comforting tastes of maple syrup and cinnamon, these roasted chickpeas are an addicting snack!

2 cups cooked chickpeas or 1 (15-ounce) can of chickpeas, rinsed and drained
2 tsp. coconut or canola oil
2 tsp. cinnamon

1 1/2 tsp. maple or coconut sugar
1/4 tsp. salt
1 Tbsp. pure maple syrup

▶ Preheat the oven to 400 degrees. Line a baking sheet with parchment paper.
▶ Remove the skins from the chickpeas as much as possible. Lightly drying them with a clean kitchen towel helps loosen them up a bit.
▶ Place the chickpeas in a bowl and add the oil, cinnamon, sugar, and salt. Toss to fully combine and lay them out on the prepared baking sheet.
▶ Place them in the oven and bake for 40 minutes or more, until desired crunch is achieved, stirring several times during baking. Remove, drizzle the maple syrup over them and toss them to fully coat each chickpea, then return to the oven for 5 more minutes. Remove from the oven and allow to cool completely before serving.

Suggestions
▶ Watch these closely so the chickpeas don't burn.

Gluten-free ▲ Quick ▲ Easy
Total time: **60 minutes**

CHOPPED VEGETABLE SALAD
WITH GINGER-TAHINI DRESSING

serves 4

I try to eat a big salad each day but sometimes I just can't face a bowl of greens staring up at me. Although this salad does include some greens, the predominant crunch comes from the vegetables—just enough to trick my mind and stomach into thinking I'm not really eating another big salad.

Salad
2 cups broccoli, cut into bite-sized pieces
1 cup cauliflower, cut into bite-sized pieces
1 yellow squash or zucchini, quartered and sliced
1/2 red bell pepper, seeded and chopped into bite-sized pieces
1 cup carrots, peeled and sliced on the diagonal
1 (15-ounce) can chickpeas, rinsed and drained
1/2 cup chopped fresh cilantro
4 cups chopped romaine lettuce
Chopped roasted peanuts or soy nuts, for garnish, optional

Dressing
1/4 cup rice vinegar
1/4 low-sodium tamari or soy sauce
1/4 cup tahini
1 Tbsp. fresh grated ginger
1/2 tsp. "prepared" horseradish (not sauce) or Dijon mustard
1/4 tsp. ground black pepper
1 small clove garlic, minced

▶ Place a steam basket in a deep pot and add about ½ inch of water. Bring the water to a boil, then turn to medium-low and place the broccoli, cauliflower, and squash or zucchini in the basket. Cover pot and cook for 5 to 8 minutes or until the vegetables are crisp-tender, but still retain their color.

▶ Meanwhile, add cold water and a handful of ice cubes to a large, deep bowl. When the vegetables are done, carefully add them to the bowl of ice water, stir, and let them sit for a few minutes to quickly cool them. Drain well and set aside.

▶ In another large bowl, add the red bell pepper, carrots, chickpeas, and cilantro. Stir in the steamed vegetables. Set aside.

Oliverio

In a small bowl, whisk together all of the dressing ingredients and pour over the vegetables in the bowl. Divide the romaine lettuce between four large bowls; divide the vegetables between the bowls and sprinkle with chopped peanuts or soy nuts, if using. Serve.

Suggestions

▶ Dry-fried or oven-baked tofu would be yummy on top of this salad.

▶ If you prefer, skip the steaming and just eat the broccoli, cauliflower, and squash raw.

▶ Mix in the romaine lettuce with the other vegetables if you'd like everything coated with dressing.

▶ Let the salad rest in the refrigerator for 30 minutes or so to really soak up the dressing.

Gluten-free ▲ High raw ▲ Oil-free ▲ Easy
Total time: **20 minutes**

CINNAMON APPLE TOAST

makes 16 large pieces

The warm smell of this thick, raw bread baking in the dehydrator is just like a slice of warm toast that has been sprinkled with cinnamon. Unlike regular toast, however, with this crunchy breakfast or snack you get essential amino and fatty acids, beta carotene, vitamins A, E, and C, potassium, fiber, and loads of other nutrients. I enjoy this coated generously in peanut butter, of course.

1 cup flaxseed meal
1/4 cup flaxseeds
1/4 cup raw sunflower seeds
1/4 cup raw hulled hemp seeds
1 1/2 tsp. cinnamon
1/4 tsp. cardamom
1/4 tsp. ground ginger
1 cup raw walnuts, soaked 8 to 12 hours, rinsed and drained

5 Medjool dates, soaked for about 15 minutes and drained
1 apple, stemmed and cored
1 small sweet potato, peeled and cut into small pieces
1/2 of a banana
1/2 cup unsweetened apple juice
1 1/2 tsp. vanilla extract
Pinch sea salt

▶ In a large bowl, whisk together the flaxseed meal, flaxseeds, sunflower seeds, hemp seeds, and spices. Set aside.

▶ Put the walnuts, dates, apple, sweet potato, banana half, apple juice, vanilla extract, and sea salt in the bowl of a food processor. Pulse until everything has been broken down into small pieces. Pour this mixture in with the flaxseed mixture and stir well to combine.

▶ Using a rubber spatula or your hands spread the dough onto a non-stick dehydrator sheet until it's about ½ inch thick. Use a knife to score the dough into 16 equal pieces. Place the sheet in the dehydrator and dry for 30 minutes at 145 degrees. Turn down the temperature to 115 degrees and continue drying until the toast is very crispy, 20 to 24 hours. After 2 to 3 hours in the dehydrator, carefully flip the toast by placing a mesh dehydrator sheet fitted into another tray on top of the dough. Flip and gently remove the non-stick sheet. Place the tray back in the dehydrator. This will speed up the drying time.

Suggestions

▶ To make thin crackers, divide the dough between two dehydrator sheets and spread to about ¼ inch thick. Score the dough and follow the instructions above. The drying time will be less, however, so be sure to check the crackers after about 12 hours.

Gluten-free ▲ Raw ▲ Oil-free ▲ Easy

Prep time: **10 minutes** *Cook time:* **20–24 hours**

GABBY'S OATMEAL CRÈME BRÛLÉE FOR ONE

serves 1

This simple, yet decadent-tasting breakfast-for-one strikes the perfect balance between healthy and indulgent. The crispness of the brûlée topping is what lands this recipe in the Crunchy chapter.

Oatmeal
1/3 cup gluten-free oats
1/3 cup Almond Milk (see recipe on page 35) or use your favorite non-dairy milk
1/3 cup water
small handful or your favorite fruit, chopped into small pieces
1 Tbsp. flaxseed meal
Your favorite sweetener, to taste, optional

Topping
1 Tbsp. hazelnuts
1 Tbsp. pumpkin seeds
1 Tbsp. sunflower seeds
1/2 Tbsp. pure maple syrup, plus extra for serving

▶ Turn your oven or toaster oven to Broil.
▶ Over medium-high heat, cook the oats in the almond milk and water, along with the fruit. You want the fruit to get soft and start to break down a little. Stir in the flax towards the end of cooking.
▶ While the oats are cooking, coarsely chop the hazelnuts and seeds.
▶ Spoon the oats into an individual-sized ramekin. Sprinkle the seeds on top and then drizzle with the ½ tablespoon maple syrup. (You could also mix the seeds with the maple syrup first then sprinkle on the topping)
▶ Place the ramekin in your oven or toaster oven and broil for 5 to 6 minutes, or until the nuts and seeds are a golden brown. Make sure to watch it as oven temperatures vary and this will quickly turn from perfectly broiled to burnt to a crisp!

Gluten-free ▲ Oil-free ▲ Quick ▲ Easy
Total time: **10 minutes**

HIGH RAW BLUEBERRY GRANOLA

makes 10 cups

If you're looking for instant granola gratification, you won't find it in this recipe. This one takes a little bit of planning, but the crunchy, sweet result is worth it. Preparation is a cinch; it's the dehydrating that takes a while.

1 cup raw sunflower seeds, soaked 8 to 12 hours, rinsed and drained
1 cup whole raw almonds, soaked 8 to 12 hours, rinsed and drained
2 cups raw pecan halves, soaked 8 to 12 hours, rinsed and drained
1 1/2 cups fresh blueberries

Zest of 1 small orange
1 apple, cored and chopped into small chunks
1 cup Date Paste (see page 40 for recipe)
1/4 cup pure maple syrup
1 tsp. cinnamon
1 tsp. vanilla extract

▶ In a food processor, pulse the sunflower seeds, almonds, and pecan halves a few times. You just want to break them down a bit. Scrape into a large bowl and add the blueberries and orange zest.

▶ Now put the apple, date paste, maple syrup, cinnamon, and vanilla extract in the food processor. Pulse a few times to combine and to break down the apple. You're not going for applesauce here—there should be small bits and pieces visible. Pour this mixture in with the nut-blueberry mixture and stir well to combine.

▶ Divide the mixture between two non-stick dehydrator sheets and dry at 115 degrees until crispy, about 48 hours. Store in an air-tight container for up to 10 days.

Suggestions

▶ Use raspberries or blackberries in place of the blueberries, or add a mixture of various berries.
▶ Try mixing up the kinds of nuts/seeds.
▶ Make this 100% raw by using agave nectar in place of the maple syrup.

Gluten-free ▲ High Raw ▲ Oil-free ▲ Easy

"PARMESAN" PITA CHIPS

makes 1 full dehydrator sheet

This is my healthy version of one of my favorite guilty cravings, Stacy's Baked Pita Chips.

1 cup raw walnuts or almonds, soaked 8
    to 12 hours, rinsed and drained
1/2 cup carrots, chopped
1 Tbsp. white miso paste
1/2 cup water
1 Tbsp. fresh lemon juice
1 tsp. dried onion flakes
1/2 tsp. garlic powder

1/4 tsp. smoked paprika
1 clove garlic
Couple of slices of red onion
1 cup flaxseed meal
1/4 cup "Parmesan" Cheez (see page 54
    for recipe), or store-bought vegan
    Parmesan cheese substitute
Pinch sea salt and black pepper

▶ In a food processor, process the walnuts, carrots, miso, water, lemon juice, onion flakes, garlic powder, smoked paprika, garlic, and red onion until smooth.

▶ Put the flaxseed meal, "Parmesan" Cheez, and salt and pepper in a bowl. Add the walnut mixture and stir thoroughly to combine. Line a dehydrator tray with a non-stick sheet and pour the dough onto the sheet. Spread the dough to about ¼ inch thick. Gently score the dough into diamonds or triangles.

▶ Set the dehydrator to 145 degrees and dry chips for 30 minutes, then turn down the heat to 115 degrees and continue dehydrating for another 12 to 24 hours. Occasionally check the consistency of the chips. After 2 to 3 hours in the dehydrator, carefully flip the chips by placing a mesh dehydrator sheet fitted into another tray on top of the dough. Flip and gently remove the non-stick sheet. Place the tray back in the dehydrator. This will speed up the drying time.

Gluten-free ▲ Raw ▲ Oil-free ▲ Easy
Prep time: **12 hours, including soak time** *Cook time:* **12–24 hours**

The day winter loosens its grip and life sprouts from the brown and dry and lifeless.
The deepest, darkest shade under a giant oak.
Cool grass between your toes.
When your body cries, "Feed me! No, really. Feed me!"
Healing, bright, cleansing, nourishing.
Green.

craving 7
GREEN

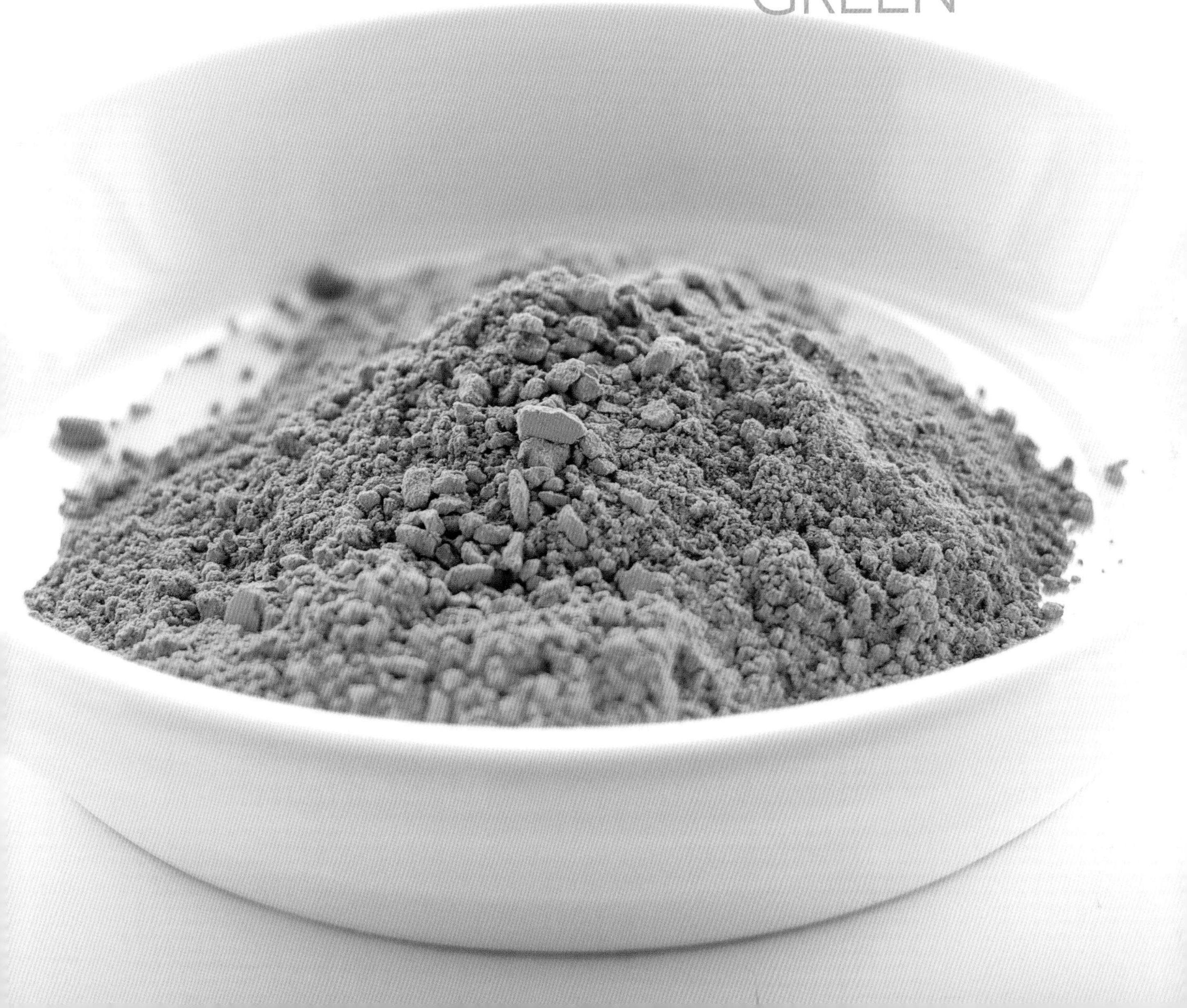

BRUSSELS SPROUTS SALAD

serves 4

Brussels sprouts look like wee cabbages growing on tall stalks. For some (like my husband), these little veggies are to be avoided at all costs, most likely because they've tried them after the sprouts have been overcooked, which brings out their bitterness and sulfurous smell. Brussels sprouts are really tasty when properly prepared, and are a good source of antioxidants like vitamins C, K, and A, so give this method a try. The key is that they aren't cooked and they're finely chopped—and they get a helping hand from tart cherries, spicy fennel, and sunny orange.

Salad
1/2 pound Brussels sprouts, trimmed
1 large head fresh fennel, roughly chopped
2 carrots, peeled and roughly chopped
1/4 cup red onion, chopped
1/2 cup dried tart cherries, roughly chopped
1 cup walnuts, toasted and chopped
8 slices Tempeh Bacon (see page 63)

Dressing
6 Tbsp. fresh orange juice
3 Tbsp. apple cider vinegar
1 tsp. Dijon mustard
1 clove garlic, minced
1/4 tsp. ground black pepper
1 tsp. fennel seeds, crushed
1 tsp. orange zest
Pinch sea salt

▶ In a large bowl, whisk together the ingredients for the dressing. Set aside.

▶ In a food processor, add the Brussels sprouts and fennel and pulse until finely chopped/shredded. Add to the bowl with the dressing. Now process the carrots and red onion and pulse until chopped into small pieces. Add the carrots and red onion to the bowl with the Brussels sprouts.

▶ Stir in the dried cherries and divide the salad between four bowls. Sprinkle the salads with the toasted walnuts and crumble 2 slices of tempeh bacon per salad on top. Serve immediately.

Suggestions
▶ Use cabbage in place of Brussels sprouts.
▶ Try using lemon juice/zest in place of orange.
▶ If you won't be serving the salad immediately, don't dress the salad. Store the salad and the dressing separately and wait until you're ready to serve before combining them.

Gluten-free ▲ Oil-free ▲ High raw ▲ Quick ▲ Easy

Total time: **10 minutes**

GENTLE GREEN SMOOTHIE

serves 2

Kel and I didn't have much success growing hardy kiwi in our garden, but thankfully, this powerhouse fruit is available year-round in grocery stores. Kiwi is loaded with fiber as well as with the antioxidant vitamin C—one hairy little fruit serving up one and a half times the recommended daily amount. They are also a source of omega-3 fatty acids which may lower the risk of heart disease and stroke.

1 cup coconut water or water
1 cup Almond Milk (see recipe on
    page 35)
1 ripe pear, cored and chopped
1 cup green grapes

2 kiwis, peeled
1 ripe banana, cut into chunks
3 large leaves kale, center ribs removed
3 ice cubes

▶ Put all ingredients into a high-speed or regular blender and process until smooth and creamy. Serve immediately.

Gluten-free ▲ Oil-free ▲ Raw ▲ Quick ▲ Easy

GREEN RICE

serves 4

1 cup brown rice
2 1/2 cups water
2 cloves garlic, minced
1 bunch fresh cilantro, chopped (about 1 cup when chopped), divided
1 tsp. salt-free herb blend, such as Mrs. Dash Original Blend

1/2 tsp. ground black pepper
Large pinch sea salt
1/2 cup chopped fresh basil leaves
1 loosely-packed cup of chopped spinach or baby kale
Juice of half a lime, or more, to taste

▸ Soak the rice in cool water for about 1 hour. Rinse several times and drain. Add the rice to a rice cooker and pour in the 2½ cups of water. Add the garlic, half of the cilantro, herb blend, black pepper and sea salt. Start the rice cooker. After it stops cooking, let the rice sit for about 10 minutes, then stir in the remaining cilantro, the basil, the spinach or kale, and the lime juice, adjust the seasonings, and serve.

Suggestions

▸ I soak and rinse the rice for two reasons: I find that it cooks faster and fluffier after a good soaking; the second reason is because of concerns about arsenic levels found in all rice—but especially in brown rice. Soaking is said to reduce arsenic levels in rice by 25 to 30%. Other recommendations are to cook rice in a much greater quantity of water than is usually done—boiling it much like one would pasta—then draining off the water when the rice is tender, and rinsing it again. Apparently brown basmati or brown jasmine rice from India and Thailand contain lower levels of arsenic than rice grown in the U.S., and rice from California has less than that grown in the southern states. If this has you feeling the heebie-jeebies, substitute another grain for the rice—or do what I do—and eat rice only a few times per month.

Gluten-free ▲ Oil-free ▲ Easy
Total time: **45 minutes**

FRENCH GREEN BEAN, ALMOND, & MUSHROOM SALAD WITH BASIL-CHIA VINAIGRETTE

serves 4

Vinaigrette
2 Tbsp. to 1/4 cup red wine vinegar
1/4 cup water
1 Tbsp. plain almond milk yogurt
1/2 Tbsp. chia seeds
1 clove garlic
1/4 tsp. Dijon mustard
6 large fresh basil leaves

Salad
4 cups (8 ounces) French green beans
   (haricots verts), ends trimmed
1/2 cup chopped roasted red peppers
1/4 cup chopped red onion
1/2 cup slivered almonds
1 1/2 cups (about 6) cremini or white
   mushrooms, finely chopped
Pinch garlic powder
Pinch ground black pepper
1 Tbsp. liquid aminos

Make the vinaigrette
▶ Combine all of the dressing ingredients in a high-speed or regular blender and process until very smooth. Set aside.

Make the salad
▶ Lightly steam the green beans in a steamer basket for about 3 minutes or until crisp-tender and still bright green. Rinse under cool water and set aside to drain well. While the green beans cook, put the chopped red onion in a small bowl and cover with cool water. Let sit for about 15 minutes, drain well. In a medium-sized bowl, combine the green beans, roasted red pepper, and the red onion. Set aside.
▶ Warm a dry skillet over medium-low heat. Add the slivered almonds and toast until light brown. Watch closely as they burn easily. Set aside to cool. Add a splash of water or vegetable broth to the skillet and add the chopped mushrooms. Sauté for about 5 minutes, or until they begin to soften and darken in color. Add the garlic powder, black pepper, and liquid aminos and stir, letting the aminos cook off. Remove mushrooms from the heat and set aside to cool for a few minutes.
▶ Add the almonds, mushrooms, and dressing to the beans. Toss well to thoroughly coat the beans. Taste and adjust seasonings and serve.

Oliverio

Suggestions

▶ You may wish to start with the smaller quantity of vinegar in the dressing and then adjust to your tastes.

▶ I suggest soaking the red onion because some don't like the strong flavor of raw onion and soaking them removes some of their bite. Leave the onion out entirely or try scallions instead, if you prefer.

Gluten-free ▲ Oil-free
Quick ▲ Easy

Total time: **30 minutes**

GREEN MATCHA & HERB SHORTBREAD

makes 16

This slightly sweet shortbread is a riff on the Gluten-free Sweet Pie Crust recipe on page 56. It's delicious alongside a bowl of soup or stew, smeared with Cashew Coconut Cream Cheez, or use it as the base for a savory pie.

These crackers get their very green hue from matcha—dried, pulverized green tea leaves. When you consume matcha powder either in tea or food form, you are eating the whole leaf rather than just the tea brewed from the leaves, so you get all of the benefits of the whole food: loads of antioxidant power. Matcha is also purported to slow the signs of aging, boost energy, and calm nerves.

1 cup Gluten-Free All-Purpose Flour Blend (see recipe on page 42) or whole wheat pastry flour
1/4 cup hazelnut or almond meal
1 Tbsp. green matcha powder (I use The Republic of Tea brand)
1 tsp. fresh thyme (or use 1/2 tsp. dried)

1 tsp. fresh rosemary (or use 1/2 tsp. dried)
Pinch sea salt
1/2 cup tahini
1 Tbsp. almond butter
1 Tbsp. pure maple syrup
4 to 5 Tbsp. ice water

▶ Preheat the oven to 425 degrees. Line a baking sheet with a parchment sheet or silicone mat.

▶ In a food processor, combine the flour, nut meal, matcha powder, herbs, and salt and pulse a few times to combine. You want to make sure that the matcha is evenly incorporated into the flour.

▶ Add the tahini, almond butter, and maple syrup and pulse a few times. With the processor running, pour in the ice water until the dough comes together and forms a sticky ball.

▶ Lightly flour a work surface and roll out the ball to a little bit thicker than ¼ inch. Using a 2-inch round cookie cutter, cut out as many circles as you can and place them on the prepared baking sheet. Squeeze the dough scraps together and roll out again. You should get 4 to 5 more circles. Place them on the cookie sheet. Using the tines of a fork, prick holes into the shortbreads.

▶ Bake the shortbreads for 15 to 20 minutes—watch them carefully because they burn quickly and easily. Remove from the pan and let cool completely on a wire rack.

Gluten-free ▲ Oil-free ▲ Quick ▲ Easy

NECTARINE OF THE GODS OVERNIGHT SMOOTHIE BOWL

serves 2 to 4

Typically, I eat a bowl of oats and a green smoothie for breakfast every weekday morning. This recipe brings them together in a very green, very delicious smoothie bowl that is a cinch to prepare and is ready in the morning when you are.

1 1/2 cups gluten-free rolled oats
1/2 cup non-dairy milk
2 nectarines, pitted and chopped
1 banana, chopped
1 cup chopped fresh pineapple or mango
1 cup fresh spinach

1 tsp. fresh lemon juice
2 Tbsp. chia seeds
1 Tbsp. superfood protein powder (I use a blend of sprouted chia, sprouted brown rice, hemp, chlorella and spirulina), optional

- ▶ Put the oats in a medium-sized bowl.
- ▶ Put all of the remaining ingredients in a high-speed or regular blender and process until very smooth. Stir this mixture into the oats, cover the bowl and place in the refrigerator overnight.
- ▶ Serve topped with fresh berries and/or chopped nuts.

Gluten-free ▲ Raw ▲ Oil-free ▲ Quick ▲ Easy ▲ Overnight
Total time: **8 minutes**

RAW/NOT RAW VEGETABLE BARLEY BOWL

serves 4

Weekends are my days for loosening up on what I eat. So on Saturday and Sundays after lunch I enjoy dessert and a big soy latte and a little something sweet post-dinner. By Sunday evening, I usually feel ready to get back into full-on healthy mode and a simple bowl filled with good grains and lots of vegetables makes me feel slightly virtuous and ready for the week ahead.

Sauce
3/4 cups raw almonds (either with skin off
    or on), or raw cashew pieces, soaked
    for 2 to 4 hours, rinsed and drained
3/4 cup light coconut milk
2 to 4 Tbsp. fresh lime juice (2 small limes)
Zest of 1 lime
1 1/4 to 1 1/2 tsp. curry powder
1 clove garlic
1 tsp. pure maple syrup
Pinch sea salt
Pinch ground black pepper
Pinch cayenne

Vegetables & Barley
4 cups cooked barley (about 1 1/4 cup
    uncooked)
5 ounces baby kale, steamed until tender

and drained
1 cup shredded, spiralized, or chopped
    zucchini (about 1/2 of 1 large squash)
1 cup shredded or spiralized carrot
    (about 2 small)
1 cup cherry tomatoes, cut in half
1 cup chopped or shredded green or
    purple cabbage

Suggested toppings
Lemon-Garlic Baked Tofu (see page 285
    for recipe), cubed
Salty & Sweet Marinated Mushrooms
    (see page 232 for recipe)
Fresh chopped cilantro
Fresh chopped basil
Fresh sprouts
Strips of seaweed snacks

— —

Make the sauce
▶ Put the sauce ingredients in a high-speed or regular blender and process until smooth. Taste and adjust the seasonings, adding more lime juice if the dressing needs more zing. Add water or more coconut milk if the sauce is too thick. Set aside.

Assemble the bowls

▶ Divide the barley between four big bowls and top with kale, zucchini, carrot, tomatoes, cabbage, and any or all of the suggested toppings. Spoon the curry sauce on top and serve.

Suggestions

▶ Use farro, brown rice, or quinoa in place of the barley.

▶ If you use almonds, you may need additional coconut milk or water.

▶ I use a quick-cooking barley from Trader Joe's that takes about 10 minutes, but regular barley is fine, too—just plan on dinner taking a little longer to prepare.

▶ The sauce will thicken as it sits so you may need to loosen it up with water.

Gluten-free ▲ High raw ▲ Oil-free ▲ Easy
Total time: **45 minutes**

SHADES OF GREEN SMOOTHIE

serves 2

An extra-green green smoothie with coconut water to refresh and hydrate naturally.

1 cup coconut water or water
1/2 English cucumber, peeled if not
    organic
1 small lime, peeled
2 kiwis, peeled
1 stalk celery, cut into chunks

1 sweet apple, cut into chunks
1/4 Date Paste (see recipe on page 40)
1 cup lightly-packed fresh mint leaves
Peppermint-flavored stevia liquid, to
    taste, optional

▶ Put all of the ingredients except for the stevia in a high-speed or regular blender. Process until smooth. Taste and add liquid stevia, if desired. Pulse a few times to incorporate the sweetener.
▶ Divide between two glasses.

Gluten-free ▲ Raw ▲ Oil-free ▲ Quick ▲ Easy
Total time: **8 minutes**

TOMATO-ZUCCHINI-BASIL PASTA

serves 4

Because the tomatoes in this dish are not cooked, you'll want to avoid hot house tomatoes. Summer supper doesn't get much easier than this.

1 (13-ounce) package gluten-free spiral pasta
4 cups very ripe tomatoes, seeded and
    chopped
1 medium-sized zucchini, cut into thin
    ribbons lengthwise
2 cloves garlic, finely minced or
    microplaned
1/2 cup chopped kalamata olives

1/4 cup capers, drained
1/4 tsp. ground black pepper
Zest of 1 lemon
1 cup fresh basil, cut into ribbons or
    chopped
"Parmesan" Cheez (see recipe on page
    54) or store-bought vegan Parmesan
    cheese substitute

▶ Cook the pasta according to package directions.
▶ While the pasta cooks, prepare the vegetables. Combine the tomatoes, zucchini, garlic, olives, capers, black pepper, and lemon zest in a large bowl.
▶ When the pasta is done, drain it well, then pour it into the bowl with the vegetables. Add the basil and then gently stir to combine. Serve with copious amounts of "Parmesan" Cheez.

Suggestions
▶ I seed the tomatoes because I find leaving them in waters down the pasta—and I don't really like the seeds in there anyway. You can skip this step if you don't mind the seeds.
▶ For extra tang, sprinkle the pasta with red wine vinegar just before serving.
▶ Make this even greener by stirring in some oil-free pesto instead of fresh basil—as one of my testers did.

Gluten-free ▲ Oil-free ▲ Quick ▲ Easy

WHITE BEAN & LOTSA KALE SOUP

serves 4 to 6

If kale and soup are your things, this one's for you. It is bursting with kale—and also with rich flavor despite the simple ingredient list. Best thing about this soup, though, is it can be prepared quickly using ingredients straight out of the pantry and freezer.

Splash of water or vegetable broth
1 large onion, diced
2 carrots, peeled and diced
2 stalks celery, chopped
3 cloves garlic, minced
1 tsp. dried thyme
1/2 tsp. ground black pepper
1 (14.5-ounce) can petite-diced tomatoes
2 (15-ounce) cans white beans or 3 cups cooked white beans

6 cups Vegetable Broth (see page 60 for recipe)
2 Red Hots Hot Dogs (see recipe on page 250) or vegan Italian sausages (such as Field Roast), chopped
1 (18-ounce) package of frozen baby kale
1/2 cup water
2 Tbsp. white miso
Sea salt, optional, to taste

- ▶ Over medium-high heat, warm a splash of water or vegetable broth in a large pot, add the onion, carrots, celery, and garlic and sauté for about 8 minutes. Add more water if the vegetables stick. Stir in the thyme and black pepper and cook an additional minute.
- ▶ Add the tomatoes, white beans and vegetable broth, Red Hots or vegan sausage, and kale. Bring to a boil and then turn the heat down to a low simmer and cook for 20 to 30 minutes.
- ▶ In a small measuring cup, whisk together the ½ cup water and miso and stir into the soup. Heat for a few more minutes then serve.

Suggestions
- ▶ Use one bunch fresh kale, chopped, instead of frozen kale.
- ▶ Add a dash of red chile pepper flakes along with the black pepper.

Gluten-free ▲ Oil-free ▲ Easy

Total time: **45 minutes**

Midnight: standing in the yellow light of the open refrigerator door,
listening to the siren call of the slice of cold pizza.
The 3 PM drop in blood sugar that sends you to the vending machine.
The crumpled, grease-stained to-go bag on the floor of the car.
Guilty, salty, sugary, satisfying.
Junk.

craving 8
JUNK

BUTTERNUT SQUASH QUESO

makes about two cups

This recipe was inspired by an appetizer at Matthew Kenney's "plant-based Mexican kitchen," Tamazul, in Oklahoma City. While everything I've eaten there has been delicious, fresh, and creative—their queso impressed me more than any other dish. I was too shy to ask how they made it, so I set about creating my own version. This also makes a delicious sauce for mac 'n' cheez.

2 cups roasted butternut squash
1/2 cup raw cashews, soaked 8 to 12
     hours, rinsed and drained
1 Tbsp. white miso paste
2 Tbsp. fresh lemon juice
1 1/2 Tbsp. nutritional yeast
1 tsp. dried onion flakes

1/2 tsp. Dijon mustard
1/2 tsp. garlic powder
1/2 tsp. smoked paprika
1/4 tsp. cumin powder
1/4 tsp. turmeric
Water, as needed

▶ Add all of the ingredients to a high-speed or regular blender and process until very smooth. You will need to tamp down the ingredients and add water—just a little at a time—during processing to get a very smooth texture.

▶ Transfer the mixture to a small saucepan and gently heat. Serve warm with Parmesan "Pita" Chips on page 180, baked tortilla chips or fresh steamed vegetables. Store leftovers in an air-tight container in the refrigerator for up to 5 days.

Suggestions

▶ Here's how I roast a butternut squash: Preheat the oven to 425 degrees and line a large baking sheet with aluminum foil. Cut off the squash's stem and pierce the skin a few times with a knife. Place the whole squash on the baking sheet and cook for 45 minutes to 1 hour, or until the flesh of the squash is very soft (I test it by inserting a knife). The skin will be shiny and dark brown. Remove from the oven and allow to cool completely before handling. Peel off the skin, then break open the squash and scoop out the seeds.

▶ Try using pumpkin purée or roasted sweet potato in place of the butternut squash.

Oliverio

- ▶ Reserve 1 cup of the queso to make Cheddar Cheez (see recipe on page 227).
- ▶ If you like it spicy, stir in a ¼ cup of fresh, diced jalapeño peppers (or pickled jalapeños)—or for milder flavor—stir in ¼ cup of roasted red bell pepper.

Gluten-free ▲ Oil-free ▲ Easy

Prep time: **10 minutes**

Cook time: **5 minutes**

COCONUT-LIME MINI DOUGHNUTS WITH COCONUT-LIME GLAZE

makes 24

Although I was never one to be tempted by those white, confectioner's sugar-dusted mini doughnuts found in vending machines and convenience stores, I'm drawn to the cuteness of anything in miniature. The flavors in these tiny cakes were inspired by the huge, moist muffins I once enjoyed from Maggie's Vegan Bakery in my hometown of Cleveland, Ohio.

Doughnuts
1/4 cup coconut oil, melted
1/4 cup unsweetened applesauce
1/4 cup Date Paste (see recipe on page 40)
1/4 cup maple sugar
2 Tbsp. fresh lime juice
Zest of 1 lime
1/4 tsp. lime oil, optional
2 2/3 cups whole wheat pastry flour
2 Tbsp. flaxseed meal
1 1/2 tsp. baking powder
1/2 tsp. sea salt
1/4 tsp. baking soda
1 cup non-dairy milk

Glaze
1/2 cup full-fat coconut milk
1/4 cup Coconut Butter, softened (see recipe on page 37)
1 Tbsp. Date Paste, or to taste
Zest of 1 lime
1/2 cup unsweetened coconut flakes, toasted

Doughnuts
▶ Preheat the oven to 425 degrees and lightly oil two 12-cup mini-doughnut pans. Set aside.
▶ In a large bowl, cream together the coconut oil, applesauce, date paste, maple sugar, lime juice, and lime zest. Set aside.
▶ In a medium-sized bowl, whisk together the whole wheat pastry flour, flaxseed meal, baking powder, sea salt, and baking soda. Stir the flour mixture into the wet ingredients, alternating with the non-dairy milk. You want to begin and end with the flour mixture. Stir well to combine thoroughly.
▶ Divide the mixture between the pans. Trying to spoon the batter perfectly into these tiny tins is maddening,

so I just plop a big spoonful of batter into each cup and go back and smooth it so that the hole is visible. Give the pans a couple of good, hard taps on the counter.

▶ Bake the doughnuts for 10 to 15 minutes, or until firm and springy to the touch. Let cool in the pans for about 10 minutes before removing them to cooling racks. Let the doughnuts cool completely before spooning on the glaze.

Glaze

▶ In a small bowl, whisk together the coconut milk, coconut butter, lime zest, and date paste. Using about half of the mixture, drizzle it over the doughnuts then sprinkle about half of the toasted coconut over top of the doughnuts. Put the doughnuts in the refrigerator for about 15 to 20 minutes, then repeat the process of drizzling with the remaining glaze and sprinkling on the remaining coconut.

▶ The glaze will not harden, but will soak into the doughnuts making them very tender and moist. Store in an air-tight container in the refrigerator for up to three days, or wrap well and store in the freezer.

Suggestions

▶ Although the lime oil is optional, it really boosts the lime flavor—so use it if you have it or can get your hands on it.

FRUIT PIZZA WITH CHOCOLATE CHIP COOKIE CRUST

serves 6 to 8

A few years back, it seemed like fruit pizzas were all the rage at baby showers and office parties. I never really got the appeal. To me, the blah sugar cookie layer was nothing but too sweet and who considered fruit a dessert anyway?! "Gimme chocolate!" I said. I've since revised my opinion. What could be more decadent than a giant chocolate chip cookie coated in rich cream cheese and topped with beautiful, juicy fresh fruit?

Cookie crust
1 Tbsp. flaxseed meal
3 Tbsp. water
1 cup plus 2 Tbsp. whole wheat pastry
   flour
1/2 tsp. baking soda
1 tsp. powdered stevia
Pinch salt
1/2 cup unsweetened applesauce
1/4 cup coconut oil, softened or melted
1/4 cup pure maple syrup
1/2 tsp. vanilla extract
1/2 cup vegan stevia-sweetened semi-
   sweet chocolate chips
1/4 cup chopped walnuts or pecans

Cream cheese layer
1/2 cup Cashew Coconut Cream Cheez
   (see recipe on page 36) or store-
   bought vegan cream cheese
1/2 Tbsp. pure maple syrup, optional

Fruit layer
1/2 cup raspberries
1 kiwi, peeled, cut in half and thinly sliced
4 strawberries, stemmed and thinly sliced
Sprig of mint

Make the cookie crust
▶ Preheat the oven to 350 degrees. Lightly spray a 9-inch pie pan with cooking oil and use a paper towel to spread the oil over the bottom and up along the sides of the pan. Set aside.
▶ Whisk together the flaxseed meal and 3 tablespoons water and set aside. In a medium-sized bowl, whisk together the flour, baking soda, stevia and salt. Set aside.
▶ In a large bowl, whisk together the flaxseed meal mixture, coconut oil, applesauce, maple syrup, and vanilla

extract. Add the flour mixture to the applesauce mixture and stir until well-combined. Fold in the chocolate chips and the nuts and spread the batter evenly along the bottom of the pie pan. Place in the oven and bake for about 25 minutes or until the cookie feels firm but springy to the touch.

▶ Allow cookie to cool in the pan for 15 minutes, then run a knife along the edges of the cookie and carefully turn it out onto a wire rack to cool completely.

Make the cream cheese layer

▶ In a small bowl, cream together the cream cheese and the maple syrup.

Assemble the pizza

▶ Spread the cream cheese on top of the cookie layer, leaving a ½-inch border of cookie. Arrange the fruit in circles around the cookie and press gently into the cream cheese. Top with a sprig of mint. Slice and serve. Store leftovers in the refrigerator.

Suggestions

▶ I use the fresh fruit I have on hand, so all kinds of other fruit would be very tasty on this as well.

▶ To make this gluten-free, use 1 cup plus 3 Tbsp. Gluten-Free All-Purpose Blend (see recipe on page 42) and add ½ tsp. xanthan gum to the baking powder, stevia, and salt listed above. Proceed with the directions.

Gluten-free Option ▲ Easy

ICED MAPLE LATTE SHAKE

serves 3 to 4

I can't help it. I cringe when I see people drinking those giant, icy, whipped cream–topped coffee confections because I can't not think about the amount of sugar in them, but . . . they sure look tasty! My solution is a quick and easy warm-weather beverage that satisfies with its smoky maple sweetness, creaminess, and just a hint of coffee flavor.

2 cups coconut or other non-dairy milk
1/4 cup pure maple syrup
2 to 3 Tbsp. herbal coffee substitute, such as Dandy Blend (or 2 Tbsp. instant coffee granules)

2 very ripe bananas, cut into chunks and frozen
1 tsp. maca powder
1/4 tsp. maple extract, optional
1 cup ice, optional

▶ Place all of the ingredients in a high-speed or regular blender and process until smooth. Serve immediately.

Suggestions
▶ This shake quickly loses its creaminess as the ice melts, so it's best sipped right away.
▶ My preference is to make this without the ice—one gets a creamier, more intense maple/coffee flavor without it—but if you like that coffee shop iciness, go for it!

Gluten-free ▲ Oil-free ▲ Quick ▲ Easy
Total time: **8 minutes**

NO-BAKE BREAKFAST COOKIES

makes 12

These are great for breakfast on the go, a mid-afternoon treat, or a post-workout snack.

1 1/2 cups old-fashioned rolled oats
1 Tbsp. teff (not teff flour)
1 Tbsp. hulled hemp seeds
1 Tbsp. chia seeds
1/2 cup dried tart cherries, roughly
    chopped

1/3 cup natural almond or peanut butter
1/2 cup unsweetened applesauce
1 Tbsp. non-dairy milk or water
1/4 tsp. vanilla-flavored liquid stevia
1 tsp. ground cinnamon

- In a food processor, pulse the oats until broken into small pieces. Pour the oats into a large bowl and add the teff, hemp seeds, chia seeds, and cherries.
- Add the nut butter, applesauce, coconut milk or water, stevia, and cinnamon to the processor bowl. Process until very smooth and scrape the mixture into the bowl with the oats. Stir until the mixture is thoroughly combined.
- Divide the oat mixture between 12 muffin cups and using damp fingers, press the mixture down to create a flat surface. Refrigerate the cookies until firm. Store in an air-tight container in the refrigerator for up to 1 week.

Suggestions
- For a chocolate cookie, omit the cinnamon and add 1 Tbsp. cacao or cocoa powder and 1 Tbsp. cacao nibs.
- Try using one ripe banana instead of the applesauce.
- Use your favorite dried fruit in place of the cherries.
- If you prefer, use maple syrup in place of the vanilla-flavored stevia. Start with 1 Tbsp. maple syrup plus ¼ tsp. vanilla extract.
- If you don't have or don't want to use teff, use additional hemp or chia seeds.

Gluten-free ▲ Oil-free ▲ Quick ▲ Easy

Junk

SOMER'S TEMPEH TACOS

serves 4

Having eaten my fair share of food prepared by Somer, my friend and blogger behind the internet phenom VedgedOut.com, I knew this recipe would be delicious. It's also an ideal weeknight meal that can be put together with a minimum of work.

Taco meat
Water or vegetable broth for sautéing
1 medium onion, finely diced
1 (8-ounce) package tempeh, grated with a box or flat grater
1 (15-ounce) can kidney beans, rinsed and drained
3/4 cup unsweetened soy or almond milk
3 Tbsp. liquid aminos
2 Tbsp. tomato paste
1 Tbsp. cacao or cocoa powder
2 tsp. chili powder
1 tsp. liquid smoke
1 heaping tsp. ground cumin
1 tsp. dried oregano
1 tsp. nutritional yeast
dash cayenne
salt and pepper to taste

Remaining ingredients
Taco shells or corn or flour tortillas
1/4 head purple cabbage, finely chopped
2 medium carrots, grated
1 sliced avocado
salsa or hot sauce
Tofu & Cashew Sour Cream (see recipe on page 61) or store-bought vegan sour cream

▶ Over medium-high heat, sauté the onion in water or vegetable broth in a large skillet until soft, about 5 minutes. Put the grated tempeh and kidney beans in a large bowl. Mix the remaining taco ingredients in a small bowl with a wire whisk. Pour liquid over the taco meat and toss to combine.

▶ Add the taco mixture to the onions. Add a little cooking oil if necessary, and stir occasionally, allowing the mixture to brown and heat through. If desired, continue to cook until the mixture gets slightly crispy, about ten minutes total.

▶ Fill tacos with the taco mixture and your preference of toppings above.

Gluten-free Option ▲ Oil-free ▲ Quick ▲ Easy

Junk

213

SPICY-COATED OVEN-BAKED VEGGIE "FRIES"

serves 4

These veggies are reminiscent of spicy-coated fries you can get at bars and restaurants—without the big helping of grease and salt. The spice mixture is very thick so you really want to get your hands in the bowl when mixing the vegetables.

1 1/2 cups broccoli, cut into bite-sized pieces
1 1/2 cups cauliflower, cut into bite-sized pieces
1 cup asparagus spears, cut into 1 1/2-inch pieces
2 Tbsp. garbanzo bean flour
1 1/2 Tbsp. nutritional yeast
1 Tbsp. fine cornmeal
1 Tbsp. flaxseed meal

1 tsp. garlic powder
3/4 tsp. baking powder
1/2 tsp. smoked paprika
1/2 tsp. chile powder
Pinch salt and ground black pepper
3 Tbsp. water
1 Tbsp. coconut oil, melted
2 tsp. Frank's Red Hot Wings Sauce (or similar "buffalo" sauce)

▶ Preheat the oven to 425 degrees and set aside a large baking sheet.
▶ In a large bowl, whisk together the garbanzo bean flour, nutritional yeast, cornmeal, flaxseed meal, garlic powder, baking powder, smoked paprika, chile powder, and salt and pepper.
▶ Stir in the water, coconut oil, and hot sauce until well-combined. Add the chopped vegetables and using your hands, mix them into the sauce, making sure to get all of the pieces coated. Place the vegetables directly on the baking sheet (do not use parchment or a silicone sheet) in one layer. Bake the vegetables for 20 to 30 minutes or until they are tender and the coating has firmed up and started to crisp. Serve immediately.

Suggestions
▶ Bump up the amount of hot sauce if you like your fries very spicy. Add cayenne or more chili powder.
▶ This coating is yummy on green beans or snap peas, too.

Gluten-free ▲ Easy
Total time: **45 minutes**

STUFFED FLATBREADS WITH CHIPOTLE-LEMON AIOLI DIP & DUNK SAUCE

makes 8

It's easy to create your own "hot pockets" that are made with whole foods and no oil. Store these individually wrapped in the freezer and gently warm for a quick lunch.

Filling

Water or vegetable broth for sautéing
1 medium bell pepper, cored, seeded and finely chopped
1 small onion, finely chopped
1 clove garlic, minced
1/4 cup of kalamata and green olives, minced, or 1/2 cup Pickled Vegetables, Olive, & Basil Tapenade (see page 230)
Pinch sea salt and ground black pepper
2 Tbsp. fresh parsley, chopped
1/2 cup shredded Cheddar Cheez (see recipe on page 227) or store-bought vegan cheese

Chipotle-Lemon Aioli Sauce

1 cup Cayonnaise (see recipe on page 38) or store-bought vegan mayonnaise
1 1/2 to 2 tsp. puréed chipotle in adobo
Zest of 1 lemon
1 tsp. fresh lemon juice
1 clove garlic, finely minced
1/4 tsp. cumin
Pinch ground black pepper

Dough

3/4 cup warm water
1/2 tsp. regular yeast
1 tsp. pure maple syrup
1 cup whole wheat flour
1 cup white whole wheat flour
1/2 tsp. sea salt
1/2 tsp. dried thyme
1/2 tsp. dried onion flakes

Make the filling

▶ Heat a skillet over medium-high heat and add a splash of water or vegetable broth. Add all of the filling ingredients except for the parsley and sauté for 8 to 10 minutes. Remove pan from the heat and stir in the parsley.

▶ Store the filling in an air-tight container in the refrigerator until you are ready to make the flatbreads.

Make the sauce

▶ Whisk together all of the sauce ingredients in a small bowl. Cover and chill until ready to use.

Make the dough

▶ Put the water, yeast, and maple syrup in the bowl of a stand mixer. Let sit for a few minutes to let the yeast bubble. Add the remaining ingredients and using the paddle attachment, process until the dough starts to come together. Put the dough hook attachment on and knead for about 6 minutes. The dough should be smooth and slightly sticky. Remove the bowl from the mixer, cover with plastic wrap and let the dough rest for 15 minutes.

▶ Line a small baking sheet with parchment paper. Divide the dough into 8 portions and roll each into a ball. Place the balls on the baking sheet, cover with plastic wrap and let rest for 30 minutes.

▶ Sprinkle a little flour on a work surface and working with one portion of dough at a time, roll each into a 6½-inch round. Place about 2 tablespoons of the filling in the center of the round. Place about 1 tablespoon of Cheddar Cheez on top of the filling. Lightly moisten the edge of the dough. Fold in the right side of the dough and then the left side. Fold in the top and then the bottom. You should end up with a fat little rectangle. Place back onto the parchment-covered baking sheet and proceed in the same manner with the remaining 7 pieces of dough.

▶ Heat a large pan or electric skillet to medium-high heat. Lightly spritz the pan/skillet with oil, turn the heat down to medium-low, and brown the flatbreads (you may only be able to fit 2 to 3 in a pan; more on an electric skillet), 4 to 5 minutes. Carefully turn the flatbreads and brown the other side. Continue in this manner until all of the flatbreads are cooked.

▶ Serve immediately with the sauce, or let cool, wrap well and store in the refrigerator or freezer until ready to serve. To reheat, remove the plastic wrap, wrap the flatbreads in foil and warm in a 350 degree oven for about 30 minutes.

Oil-free
Total time: **90 minutes, including rise time**

Junk

WHOLE GRAIN PRETZEL TWISTS

makes 36

Shopping mall or airport cinnamon rolls never really appealed to me—something about the artificial smell of them turned me off. But I did love hot, soft pretzels sprinkled with big chunks of salt. I haven't had one in years, but that doesn't mean I lost my love for the yeasty, slightly bitter flavor of soft pretzels. Instead of kosher salt, I've sprinkled mine with a combination of seeds, but if you enjoy salt—add a little bit to the seed mixture.

1 cup warm water
2 1/4 tsp. active dry yeast
2 Tbsp. pure maple syrup
2 cups whole wheat flour
3/4 cup light rye flour
2 Tbsp. vital wheat gluten
1 Tbsp. maca powder or 1/4 cup barley
    malt powder

1 tsp. sea salt
Fine cornmeal, for dusting baking pans
1/4 cup baking soda
1 Tbsp. sesame seeds
1 Tbsp. chia seeds
1 Tbsp. poppyseeds

▶ In the bowl of a stand mixer, combine the water, yeast, and maple syrup. Let sit for a few minutes until bubbly. Meanwhile, in a medium-sized bowl, whisk together the flours, vital wheat gluten, maca powder (or barley malt powder), and salt.

▶ Pour the flour mixture into the yeast mixture and using the paddle attachment, mix at low speed until a dough is formed. Now switch to the hook attachment and knead the dough for about 10 minutes. If the dough is too sticky, add small amounts of flour until a ball is formed. The dough should feel tacky to the touch, but shouldn't stick.

▶ Lightly oil a large bowl and add the dough, turning to coat. Cover the bowl with plastic wrap and let rise for about 1 hour. Line two baking sheets with silicone or parchment and sprinkle lightly with cornmeal. In a small bowl, combine the sesame seeds, chia seeds, and poppy seeds. Set aside.

▶ When the dough has risen to about double its original size, remove it from the bowl and knead it a few times on a lightly floured surface. Divide the dough into 8 equal pieces. Working with one piece at a time, roll into a 16- to 18-inch piece, then cut into 4 equal pieces. Roll each of the four pieces into 8-inch lengths. Again, working with one piece at a time, fold into a U-shape and then twist one or two times. You should have a shape something like a breast cancer ribbon. Twist the 3 other pieces in the same manner and place them on the prepared baking sheet. Continue in this manner—rolling the large dough pieces into 18-inch lengths, cutting those lengths into 8-inch pieces, folding and twisting until you've used up all of the dough pieces. You should end up with a total of 36 twists/ribbons.*

▶ Lightly spritz the twists with cooking oil, cover and let rise for 1 hour. Preheat the oven to 425 degrees.

▶ While the oven heats, fill a large pot with 10 to 12 cups of water. Bring the water to a boil. Once the pretzels have risen and the oven is at temperature, carefully add the ¼ cup of baking soda to the water. The water will bubble up and briefly turn white. Working with 5 to 6 pretzels at a time, carefully add them to the pot. Count to 30 and flip the pretzels, counting to 30 again. Using a slotted spoon, remove the pretzels from the water and place them back on the baking sheet. Add another 5 to 6 pretzels to the water—again, cooking each about 30 seconds per side before returning them to the baking sheet. When all of the pretzels have been boiled, sprinkle them with the seed mixture.

▶ Place the baking sheets in the oven and bake the pretzels for 10 to 12 minutes, or until nicely browned. Switch pans about halfway through for even baking and browning. Let the pretzels cool slightly before eating, or let cool completely, wrap well and freeze for later. Popping them briefly in a toaster oven crisps them right up after thawing.

Suggestions
▶ For a more authentic pretzel taste, use barley malt syrup in place of the maple syrup.
▶ Serve these with Chipotle Cheez Sauce or Butternut Queso.

*At this point, you can place the twists in the refrigerator to rest overnight—just as is done when making bagels. Lightly spritz the twists with cooking oil, cover, and put in the refrigerator. The next day, take the twists out of the refrigerator and let them warm up for about an hour before proceeding with the recipe.

Oil-free

Total time: **3 hours**

SWEET POTATO FRIES WITH GARLIC, LEMON, & PARSLEY

serves 4

Homely tubers, sweet potatoes nevertheless come with some great benefits besides their versatility and natural sweetness. The bright orange or yellow color lets you know that they contain beta-carotene—a flavonoid that our bodies convert into vitamin A. We need vitamin A for healthy skin, for strengthening our immune system, and for good eye health.
This simple side dish is so easy to prepare, but it's bursting with delicious flavor.

2 large sweet potatoes, peeled, and cut
    into strips (like French fries)
1 Tbsp. coconut oil

1 clove garlic, minced
1/2 cup fresh parsley, chopped
Zest of 1 lemon

▶ Preheat oven to 425 degrees and line a baking sheet with parchment paper.
▶ Spread sweet potato strips onto the pan in a single layer and bake for about 15 minutes. Turn the slices and continue to bake until they are soft and beginning to brown.
▶ While the sweet potatoes bake, put the coconut oil in a deep skillet and add the garlic. Just before the fries are done, gently sauté the garlic in the oil until fragrant. Add the fries and stir, coating them with the oil and garlic. Remove the pan from the heat and stir in the parsley and lemon zest. Serve immediately.

Suggestions
▶ Try using lime instead of lemon, and cilantro in place of the parsley.

Gluten-free ▲ Quick ▲ Easy

Cook time: **15 minutes**

Shiny crystals on a warm soft pretzel.
A mouthful of the Pacific Ocean.
A bowl of miso soup swirling with seaweed.
Pass the chips, please.
Thirsty, saline, briny, shake-shake.
Salty.

craving 9
SALTY

ASHLEE'S SMOKY EGGPLANT STEAKS WITH BALSAMIC CASHEW CREAM & PINE NUTS

serves 2

Ashlee developed this recipe for the Chicago-based meal delivery service, Home Chef, and the ease of preparation and richness of flavor make this a weeknight favorite.

Eggplant is low in calories, but rich in fiber, minerals like potassium and magnesium, as well as B vitamins, folate, and vitamin C. Choose eggplants that are on the small side (less seeds mean less bitter taste) and shiny with no bruises or soft spots.

1 medium-sized eggplant, ends trimmed
2 garlic cloves, minced
2 sprigs fresh parsley, minced
Juice of 1 lemon
1/2 cup raw cashew pieces
1/8 cup pine nuts

2 Tbsp. liquid smoke
1 Tbsp. balsamic vinegar, divided
1 Tbsp. smoked paprika
Sea salt and pepper, to taste
2 cups fresh arugula

Prep the ingredients

▶ Preheat the oven to broil and lightly spray a baking sheet with cooking oil, spreading it evenly with a paper towel. Rinse and cut the eggplant lengthwise into four ½-inch slices. Dry with a paper towel. Mince the garlic and the parsley. Place the cashews in a small bowl, cover with cool water, and let soak for 20 minutes.

▶ Heat a small skillet over medium heat. Add the pine nuts and stir to prevent burning. After about 3 minutes the pine nuts should be browned and aromatic. Remove pan from the heat and set aside.

Marinate and broil the eggplant

▶ In a large, shallow dish, whisk together the liquid smoke, 1 teaspoon of the balsamic vinegar (reserving the remainder for the cashew cream), smoked paprika, garlic, salt and pepper to taste. Place the eggplant steaks in the marinade and let rest for 15 minutes.

▶ After 15 minutes, place the eggplant steaks on the prepared baking sheet. Broil for 4 to 5 minutes. Remove from the oven and brush with the remaining marinade. Broil for an additional 4 to 5 minutes.

Make the cashew cream

▶ Drain and rinse the cashews. Place them in a blender with fresh water to cover by ½ inch and blend on high until smooth and creamy. Add a tablespoon more of water if necessary. Gradually add the reserved balsamic vinegar and the lemon juice. Taste and adjust the seasoning with sea salt and pepper, if desired. Place the cashew cream in the refrigerator until ready to serve.

▷ Arrange arugula (1 cup per plate) on two plates. Top the arugula with one eggplant slice per plate and drizzle with cashew cream. Top with another eggplant slice and more cashew cream. Garnish with toasted pine nuts and serve.

Gluten-free ▲ Quick ▲ Easy

Total time: **35 minutes**

CHEDDAR CHEEZ

makes about 2 1/2 cups

If you have a batch of Butternut Squash Queso already made, this "hard" cheez comes together in minutes. Feel free to leave out the coconut oil—the cheez will taste just as yummy—but it won't have that meltability factor.

1 cup Butternut Squash Queso (see
    recipe on page 204)
1 Tbsp. coconut oil, melted, optional
1 1/2 Tbsp. nutritional yeast
1/4 tsp. smoked paprika

Pinch sea salt, optional
1 tsp. fresh lemon juice plus pinch citric
    acid
1 1/2 cups water
6 Tbsp. (5 ounces) agar agar flakes

Prep the ingredients

▶ Have 3 or 4 small ungreased ramekins ready.
▶ Put the queso, coconut oil, nutritional yeast, smoked paprika, sea salt, if using, and lemon juice and citric acid in a high-speed or regular blender.
▶ In a small saucepan bring the water to a boil and add the agar agar flakes. Turn the heat down to a simmer and whisk the mixture. Simmer for 5 minutes, whisking occasionally, or until the agar flakes have completely dissolved.
▶ With the blender on low, carefully pour in the agar mixture. When it's all been added, cover the blender and process until the mixture is very smooth and everything is combined. Divide the cheez between the ramekins and place them in the refrigerator until the cheez has set, 2 to 4 hours.

Suggestions
▶ Add chopped pimiento, red pepper flakes or jalapeño peppers.

Gluten-free ▲ Oil-free option ▲ Easy
Total time: **5 minutes + 3 hours setting time**

MISO-BRAISED BUTTERNUT SQUASH

serves 4

I'm not big on making side dishes, but when it comes with B vitamins, fiber, beneficial bacteria, and anti-inflammatory properties—I'm in!

1 (1-pound) butternut squash, peeled and cut into bite-sized pieces
1 cup Vegetable Broth (see page 60 for recipe) or use store-bought low-sodium broth, divided

1/2 cup light coconut milk
1 Tbsp. fresh ginger, grated
3 cloves garlic, minced
1/4 cup white miso paste

▶ In a bowl, whisk together ½ cup of the vegetable broth, coconut milk, ginger, and garlic.
▶ Place the squash pieces into a large skillet and pour the sauce over it. Bring the mixture to a boil, reduce the heat to medium-low, cover and cook for 15 to 20 minutes or until the squash is tender.
▶ Whisk the miso into the remaining ½ cup of vegetable broth, pour into the skillet and cook for an additional minute. Serve immediately.

Gluten-free ▲ Oil-free ▲ Quick ▲ Easy
Prep time: **10 minutes** *Cook time:* **20 minutes**

QUICK MISO SOUP FOR TWO

serves 2

This is the soup I crave when I'm feeling under the weather. The bite of the fresh ginger and the natural saltiness of the miso feel so soothing on a sore throat. Mushrooms are a delicious way to get vitamins D2 and D3—and they also strengthen our immune system.

2 1/2 cups water
4 to 5 cremini mushrooms, stemmed and
    thinly sliced
6 tsp. white miso paste
1/2-inch piece of fresh ginger, peeled

1 small clove garlic
10 leaves baby spinach
2 scallions, chopped, for garnish
Seaweed strips, for garnish

▶ Bring the water to a boil in a small pot or tea kettle. Then let sit to cool down a bit as you prepare the remaining ingredients.

▶ Sauté the mushrooms in a splash of water or vegetable broth over medium-high heat. Stir occasionally. Let the broth cook off so that the mushrooms brown, 6 to 8 minutes. Set aside.

▶ Divide the miso paste between two small bowls. Pour 1¼ cups of the hot water in each bowl and whisk to fully dissolve the miso. Grate half of the ginger into one bowl; grate the remaining half in the other bowl. Do the same with the garlic. Snip the spinach into strips—5 leaves per bowl. Add the mushrooms and a sprinkle of scallions and seaweed strips, if using, to the top of each bowl of soup. Serve.

Suggestions
▶ Miso types and brands vary in flavor and intensity. Taste the soup before serving and add more miso, if necessary.

Gluten-free ▲ Oil-free ▲ Quick ▲ Easy

Salty

PICKLED VEGETABLES, OLIVE, & BASIL TAPENADE

makes 2 cups

This makes a flavorful, salty dip for breads and crackers, but I especially enjoy it as a sandwich spread with fresh tomato slices and roasted vegetables.

1 (16-ounce) bottle pickled vegetables
    (a.k.a. giardiniera), drained
1/2 cup pitted kalamata olives
1 cup loosely packed fresh basil leaves

1 clove garlic
7 to 8 fresh mint leaves
1/4 tsp. ground black pepper

▶ Put all ingredients in the bowl of a food processor and pulse until everything is uniformly and finely chopped. Taste and adjust seasonings.

▶ Store in an air-tight container in the refrigerator for 10 to 14 days.

Gluten-free ▲ Oil-free ▲ Quick ▲ Easy
Total time: **5 minutes**

SALTY & SWEET MARINATED BAKED MUSHROOMS

makes about 1 cup

These highly-flavored mushrooms aren't meant for eating on their own, but rather as an addition to sandwiches, stir-fries, and pastas.

1/2 cup Vegetable Broth (see page 60 for recipe) or low-sodium vegetable broth from a carton
2 Tbsp. low-sodium tamari, soy sauce, or liquid aminos
1 Tbsp. mild white miso paste
1 1/2 to 2 Tbsp. pure maple syrup
1 tsp. smoked paprika

1 tsp. "prepared" horseradish (not sauce or dressing)
1 tsp. Dijon mustard
1/2 tsp. dried onion flakes
1/2 tsp. ground black pepper
1/4 tsp. garlic powder
16-ounces cremini mushrooms, stemmed and cut into 1/4-inch slices

▶ In a large bowl, whisk together all of the ingredients except for the mushrooms. Add the mushrooms and stir, making sure all of the mushrooms are coated with the marinade. Let sit for about 30 minutes, stirring occasionally.

▶ Preheat the oven to 425 degrees. Spread the mushrooms with all of the marinade onto a large baking sheet. Bake for 25 to 35 minutes, stirring occasionally, until the mushrooms begin to brown and most of the marinade has evaporated.

▶ Serve immediately or store in the refrigerator for up to 3 days.

Suggestions
▶ Use button mushrooms instead of cremini.

Gluten-free ▲ Oil-free ▲ Quick ▲ Easy
Total time: **45 minutes**

UMAMI GREENS (GARLICKY SAUTÉED GREENS)

serves 2 to 3

I always have a few bags of frozen greens in the freezer for when I need a quick side dish—and this is about as quick and simple as they come. I like to eat these greens alongside Creamy Scrambled Tofu (see recipe on page 115), on top of rice and beans, or with stir-fries. If you like a little heat, add red pepper flakes when sautéing the garlic, or add a dash of cayenne pepper.

A quick primer on umami. So there's sweet, salty, sour, and bitter—and then there's this additional savory taste going on that the Japanese identified and is associated with amino acids. It translates to "delicious taste." I'll second that!

Water or vegetable broth for sautéing
1 (18-ounce) package frozen baby
    kale, or other mild-tasting greens
    (beet greens are quite nice) or 2
    medium-sized bunches of fresh kale,
    chopped

2 cloves garlic, minced
2 plus tsp. liquid aminos
Ground black pepper, to taste

▶ Put the greens in a medium-sized pot and add a splash of water or broth. Cook over medium heat for about 20 minutes, stirring occasionally and adding small amounts of water if the pan dries out. After 15 minutes, stir in the garlic with another small splash of water or broth.

▶ Sauté for 1 minute or until the garlic is fragrant. Cook off as much water as you can and add the liquid aminos and black pepper. Stir for another minute or two. Top with more liquid aminos, if desired. Serve.

Suggestions
▶ Sprinkle with "Parmesan" Cheez (see recipe on page 54) right before serving.

Gluten-free ▲ Oil-free ▲ Quick ▲ Easy
Total time: **25-30 minutes**

Salty

TOFU GYROS WITH TZATZIKI

serves 4

Gyros were my kryptonite before I went vegan. Despite being a little bit afraid of the mystery meat on a revolving skewer, I couldn't resist these salty sandwiches wrapped in warm pitas and smothered in tangy tzatziki. When I gave up animal products, I knew that I had to recreate gyros or die trying. Thankfully, I'm still here. With vegan gyros in hand.

This is a make-ahead meal where most of the work happens in the refrigerator. If you plan ahead, it makes an easy and satisfying weeknight meal.

Tofu

12-ounces extra firm tofu, pressed and drained
2 cloves garlic, minced
1/2 Tbsp. garlic powder
1 1/2 tsp. dried oregano
1 tsp. dried onion flakes
1 tsp. sea salt
1 tsp. ground black pepper
1 tsp. dried thyme
7 Tbsp. Vegetable Broth (see recipe on page 60) or store-bought low-sodium vegetable broth
2 Tbsp. liquid aminos
1 tsp. white wine vinegar
2 Tbsp. fresh lemon juice

Tzatziki

1 cup raw cashew pieces, soaked for a few hours, rinsed and drained
1/2 tsp. garlic powder
1 clove garlic
1 tsp. dried onion flakes
1/4 tsp. sea salt
1/4 tsp. dried mustard powder
1/4 cup Vegetable Broth
1 Tbsp. white wine vinegar
1 Tbsp. plus 1 tsp. fresh lemon juice
1/2 medium-sized cucumber, peeled, seeded, and chopped
1/2 tsp. dried dill weed
4 whole wheat or gluten-free pitas or tortillas
Chopped kalamata olives, for topping
Chopped fresh tomato, for topping
Chopped romaine lettuce, for topping
Sliced red onion, for topping
Chopped parsley or cilantro, for topping

Marinate the tofu

▶ Cut the block of tofu into thin slices, per the instructions on pages 30 and 31.
▶ Combine the garlic through the lemon juice in a shallow baking dish. Add the tofu slices and turn to coat. Cover the dish with plastic wrap and place in the refrigerator to marinate overnight, turning the pieces once or twice.

Make the tzatziki

▶ Combine all of the ingredients except for the cucumber and dill in a high-speed or regular blender. Process until smooth and creamy. Scrape the mixture into a small bowl and stir in the cucumber and dill weed. Cover and place in the refrigerator for a couple of hours or overnight.

Make the gyros

▶ The next day, preheat the oven to 425 degrees and bake the tofu for 45 to 60 minutes, turning the slices once or twice. Add splashes of water or vegetable broth when the liquid bakes off. Bake until the tofu begins to brown and firms. Remove from the oven.
▶ Warm the pitas or tortillas. Divide the tofu between the pitas or tortillas and top with olives, tomato, lettuce, onion, and parsley and/or cilantro. Serve with big dollops of tzatziki.

Suggestions

▶ Though I prefer tofu, these can also be made with strips of tempeh. Instructions for marinating and baking are the same.
▶ To save time, use Tofu & Cashew Sour Cream (see recipe on page 61) as the tzatziki base if you have some on hand, or use store-bought vegan sour cream. Stir in the cucumber, dill weed and a pinch of black pepper and you're good to go.

Gluten-free ▲ Oil-free ▲ Easy

Prep time: **24 hours** *Cook time:* **1 hour**

Late August, fanning yourself with a folded
newspaper because the A/C is broken.
A double-dog-dare-you to add a big glug of habanero
hot sauce to your bowl at the annual chili cook-off.
A lit firecracker.
Hot, peppery, five-alarm, red alert.
Spicy.

craving 10
SPICY

ALEX'S SPICY MUSHROOM LETTUCE CUPS

serves 4

Mushrooms are a fungi powerhouse! They are a good source of iron, calcium and vitamin D and B2 (although not button or white mushrooms). Alex uses a small amount of sesame oil in this for its distinct flavor. However, if you want to stick with only coconut oil, that's fine, it just won't be as sesame-y!

16 butter lettuce leaves, or boston bibb, collard leaves or romaine lettuce
2 tsp. coconut oil, divided
1 large onion, chopped
10-ounces cremini or button mushrooms, finely chopped
2 cloves garlic, minced
1 Tbsp. low-sodium tamari or soy sauce
2 Tbsp. rice wine vinegar
2 tsp. minced ginger

1 Tbsp. Asian chile sauce, or to taste
1/4 cup homemade hoisin sauce (see recipe below)
1 (8-ounce) can water chestnuts, drained and finely chopped
1/2 cup chopped scallions
1 tsp. toasted sesame oil, optional
1/2 cup shredded carrots
2 tbsp. sesame seeds, lightly toasted

▶ In a large skillet (preferably cast iron), heat 1 teaspoon coconut oil over medium heat. Add the onion and cook until soft, about 5 minutes. Remove the onion from the pan and add the other teaspoon coconut oil along with the mushrooms. Spread the mushrooms out. This will allow them to get crispy without steaming them. Let cook until reduced and browned, about 7 minutes. Add the onion back to the pan along with the garlic and stir together.

▶ Whisk together the soy sauce, rice wine vinegar, ginger, chile sauce, and hoisin sauce. Add to the mushrooms along with the water chestnuts and chopped scallions. Stir to combine and cook an additional 2 to 3 minutes until warmed through and onions are slightly wilted. Remove from heat and stir in sesame oil.

▶ To serve, spoon mushroom filling into lettuce cups. Garnish with shredded carrots and lightly toasted sesame seeds.

Gluten-free ▲ Oil-free Option ▲ Easy

Total time: **30 minutes**

Oliverio

HOMEMADE HOISIN SAUCE

1 tsp. oil
1/2 tsp. minced garlic
1/4 tsp. Chinese five-spice powder
1/4 cup white miso paste

1/4 cup maple syrup
1 Tbsp. rice vinegar
1/8 tsp. Sriracha sauce

▶ In a small saucepan, heat the oil over medium heat. Add the minced garlic and five-spice powder. Stir together, being careful not to brown—about 15 seconds. Add the remaining ingredients and whisk until smooth. Continue to cook over medium heat until thickened, about 5 minutes. Remove from heat and let cool.

Suggestions
▶ Make this oil-free by using water or vegetable broth for sautéing the onion and mushrooms. And just omit the oil in the hoisin sauce.
▶ You can use store-bought hoisin sauce, but it usually contains high fructose corn syrup.

BUCKWHEAT NOODLES WITH SPICY ALMOND SAUCE

serves 4

Sauce

4 Tbsp. natural almond butter
1 Tbsp. white miso paste
1/4 cup Vegetable Broth (see recipe on page 60) or store-bought low-sodium broth
1/4 cup rice wine vinegar
1/4 tsp. garlic chile paste
Juice of 1 lime
2 Tbsp. tamari, soy sauce, or liquid aminos
2 tsp. pure maple syrup
1 Tbsp. fresh ginger, grated or minced
3 cloves garlic
Pinch of ground black pepper

Noodles

6-ounces buckwheat noodles
2 cups asparagus, cut into 1-inch pieces
2 cups snow peas
1 small zucchini, cut into 1/4-inch rounds
1/4 cup red onion, chopped
1 cup grated carrot
1/2 cucumber, seeded and chopped
Fresh cilantro, for garnish
Fresh mint, for garnish
Chopped roasted peanuts, for garnish

▶ Fill a large pot with water and bring to a boil. Lightly cook the asparagus, snow peas and zucchini for about 3 minutes. You want the vegetables to retain their crunch and bright color. Using a slotted spoon, remove the vegetables and rinse with cool water—or if desired, place the vegetables in a water/ice bath for a few minutes. Drain thoroughly and set aside.

▶ Now add the buckwheat noodles to the boiling water and cook according to package directions. Drain and set aside.

▶ To make the sauce, place all of the sauce ingredients in a high-speed or regular blender and process until very smooth. If desired, thin out the sauce with additional vegetable broth or water.

▶ Combine the sauce with the noodles, the cooked vegetables and the red onion, carrot, and cucumber, and top with cilantro, mint, and peanuts.

Gluten-free ▲ Oil-free ▲ Easy

Prep time: **10–15 minutes** *Cook time:* **10 minutes**

CHIPOTLE CHEEZ SAUCE

makes 1 1/2 cups

This sauce comes together in minutes and if you process it long enough in the blender, it will warm up nicely. It doesn't melt or stretch like real cheese, but with no oil or dairy, this whole food sauce healthfully satisfies those cheesy-spicy cravings.

If you like a slightly thicker, creamier sauce, add about ¼ cup raw cashews that have been soaked for a few hours.

1 cup roasted butternut squash
1/2 cup non-dairy milk
2 Tbsp. nutritional yeast
1/2 Tbsp. fresh lemon juice
1/2 Tbsp. white wine vinegar
1 tsp. white miso
1/2 tsp. onion flakes

1/4 tsp. garlic powder
1/4 tsp. chipotle chili powder (or additional chipotle in adobo)
1/4 tsp. cumin
1/4 tsp. puréed chipotle in adobo sauce
Pinch turmeric
Pinch sea salt

▶ Combine all ingredients in a high-speed or regular blender and process until very smooth.
▶ Store in an air-tight container for up to 1 week.

Suggestions
▶ Yummy on top of a big bowl of rice and beans, a pile of nachos, as a quick chip dip, inside a burrito, or smeared on a sandwich.

Oliverio

Gluten-free ▲ Oil-free ▲ Quick ▲ Easy

GREEN CHILE CHIPOTLE CILANTRO DRESSING

makes 2 cups

1/4 cup apple cider vinegar
1/2 cup water
1/2 cup lager beer, water or Vegetable
 Broth (see recipe on page 60), or
 store-bought low-sodium broth
1/2 cup raw cashew pieces
1/4 cup pepitas
Juice of 1 lime
2 oz. chopped green chiles
1 tsp. cumin

1/2 tsp. Chipotle Tabasco Sauce, or more,
 to taste
1/8 to 1/4 tsp. chile powder
1/8 tsp. coriander
Pinch sea salt and black pepper
Small handful of cilantro
1/2-inch piece of turmeric root, peeled or
 1/4 tsp. dried turmeric
1 clove garlic
1 Medjool date

▶ Combine all of the ingredients in a high-speed or regular blender and process until smooth.

Gluten-free ▲ Oil-free ▲ Quick ▲ Easy
Total time: **5 minutes**

Spicy

CHIPOTLE SALSA

makes about 1 cup

I'm addicted to the chipotle salsa made by a certain big box store that shall remain unnamed. It's really good! I wanted to see if I could come up with an oil-free copycat and happily, I'm just as addicted to my homemade version. Serve with chips, of course, or add to burritos or a bowl of rice and beans. If you're serving a crowd, double or triple this recipe.

1 cup canned crushed tomatoes
1 jalapeño pepper, stemmed, seeded and cut in half
1 red bell pepper, stemmed, seeded and cut in half
1 clove garlic, roughly chopped
Juice of 1 lime
1/2 tsp. white vinegar

1/2 tsp. chili powder
1/4 tsp. garlic powder
1/4 tsp. cumin
1/4 tsp. smoked paprika
1/4 plus tsp. chipotle in adobo
Pinch sea salt
1 plus Tbsp. fresh chopped cilantro, optional

▶ Line a baking sheet with foil and place the jalapeño and bell pepper on the foil. Press down on the pepper halves to flatten them slightly. Place an oven rack in the highest position and turn on the broiler. Put the peppers in the oven and broil for 8 to 10 minutes, or until most of the skin on the peppers is blackened and charred. Watch closely! You may want to leave the oven door partly open. When the peppers are nicely charred, use tongs to put them inside of a paper bag and scrunch the bag closed. Let the peppers sit for 10 to 15 minutes. Take the peppers out of the bag and allow them to cool before handling. Remove the skins and discard. Roughly chop the peppers and set aside.

▶ In a food processor or blender, combine the crushed tomatoes, roasted peppers, and the remaining ingredients. Pulse or process until it's fairly smooth, but with a few small chunks—or to the texture of your liking. Stir in the chopped cilantro, if using, and serve alongside Parmesan "Pita" Chips (see recipe on page 180) or baked tortilla chips.

Gluten-free ▲ Oil-free ▲ Easy
Total time: **25 minutes**

Spicy

CREAMY THAI CARROT COCONUT SOUP

serves 4

Water or vegetable broth for sautéing
1 large onion, roughly chopped
7 to 8 large carrots, roughly chopped (no
    need to peel if organic)
4 cloves garlic, peeled
1 Tbsp. coconut oil, melted
Garlic powder and ground black pepper
1 tsp. garam masala
1 tsp. curry powder
1/4 tsp. turmeric

1/4 tsp. ground ginger
Pinch cayenne, or to taste
4 cups unsalted Vegetable Broth (see
    page 60 for recipe) or store-bought
    low-sodium broth
1 (13.6-ounce) can light coconut milk
1/3 cup fresh orange juice
Diced cucumber
Minced cilantro
Chopped peanuts

▶ Preheat the oven to 425 degrees. In a large bowl, combine the onion, carrots, garlic, and melted coconut oil, sprinkle with garlic powder and pepper and toss to coat. Transfer the vegetables to a large baking pan. Roast for 45 minutes or until the carrot and onion begin to soften and the edges get browned, turning them once or twice.

▶ In a large pot, add a splash of water or vegetable broth and set heat to medium. Add the carrot mixture and cook for a few minutes. Stir in the garam masala, curry powder, turmeric, ginger, cayenne, and black pepper and cook for another minute.

▶ Pour in the vegetable broth, bring the soup to a boil, reduce the heat to a simmer and cover the pot. Cook for 45 minutes. The carrots should be very tender.

▶ Carefully add the soup to a blender and process until very smooth. You may need to do this in batches. Put the soup back in the pot and stir in the coconut milk and orange juice. Gently reheat, stirring occasionally.

▶ To serve, divide soup between four bowls and garnish with cucumber, cilantro, and peanuts.

Suggestions
▶ Instead of carrots, try roasted sweet potato or pumpkin.

Gluten-free ▲ Easy

Prep time: **10 minutes** *Cook time:* **90 minutes**

Oliverio

246

JALAPEÑO HOT SAUCE

makes 1 cup

My heat-o-meter is pretty low; even some mild salsas make me sweat. This hot sauce is not for the faint of heart. But I know there are many out there who seek out the hottest of condiments. Be sure to use gloves when cleaning the jalapeños. You do not want to accidentally rub your eyes after handling them! If you can handle the heat, you'll benefit from the jalapeños' dose of vitamins A and C.

1/2 pound jalapeño peppers
1 small green bell pepper, stemmed,
    seeded and cut in half
1/2 cup distilled white vinegar
2 Tbsp. water

1/4 tsp. sea salt
1/8 tsp. ground black pepper
1 tsp. liquid aminos
1/2 to 1 tsp. Date Paste (see recipe on
    page 40)

▸ Set the broiler to 500 degrees and put the oven rack at the highest level. Line a baking sheet with aluminum foil and place the jalapeños and green bell pepper halves on the sheet.

▸ Broil for 5 minutes, watching carefully. You want the skin to be blackened and blistered. Remove the baking sheet and turn the peppers over to broil the other side. Broil an additional 5 minutes. Take the pan out of the oven and using tongs, place the peppers in a paper bag, seal, and let sit for 5 minutes or so.

▸ Open the bag and let the peppers cool slightly. When you can handle them comfortably, use rubber or latex gloves to remove the skins from the peppers. Slice open the jalapeños to clean out the seeds and ribbing. Add the peppers to a blender or food processor.

▸ Add the remaining ingredients to the food processor and process until smooth. If you like, pour the sauce through a fine-meshed strainer; you'll get about ¼ cup less, but will have a silkier sauce. Store in an air-tight container in the refrigerator indefinitely.

Gluten-free ▲ Oil-free ▲ Easy
Total time: **20 minutes**

Spicy

RED HOTS (SPICY SEITAN HOT DOGS)

makes 6

If you've never made your own hot dogs, now is the time to roll up your sleeves and get after it! Yeah, that's a long list of ingredients down there and there are a couple of steps, but it's super easy and the effort is well-worth the result. Not only because these taste great, have a similar texture to meat hot dogs—but because you control what goes into them. There's nothing funky (like Pink Slime) in these babies.

Bouillon
1 cup hot water
1 Tbsp. salt-free herb blend such as Mrs. Dash Original Blend
1 Tbsp. red miso paste
1 Tbsp. Spicy Catsup (see recipe on page 253) or tomato paste
1 tsp. liquid smoke
2 to 3 tsp. Sriracha, or your favorite hot sauce
1 Tbsp. finely minced onion
3 cloves garlic, grated or finely minced

Hot dogs
1 cup vital wheat gluten
1/3 cup rolled oats
1 Tbsp. nutritional yeast
Dash red pepper flakes

Spice Blend
1 tsp. garlic powder
1 tsp. dried onion flakes
1/2 tsp. dried marjoram
1/2 tsp. yellow or black mustard seeds
1/2 tsp. smoked paprika
1/2 tsp. ground black pepper
1/4 tsp. ground coriander
Pinch sea salt
Pinch cayenne

Broth
1 1/2 cups water
1 1/2 cups Vegetable Broth (see page 60 for recipe), or store-bought low-sodium broth
1 Tbsp. low-sodium tamari, or liquid aminos
-OR-
3 cups water

- In a small bowl, whisk together the bouillon ingredients: the hot water, herb-blend, miso paste, Spicy Catsup or tomato paste, liquid smoke, Sriracha, minced onion, and garlic. Stir well to combine. Set aside.
- In a large bowl, whisk together the hot dog ingredients: vital wheat gluten, rolled oats, nutritional yeast, and red pepper flakes. Set aside.
- In a spice grinder, combine the spice blend ingredients—garlic powder, onion flakes, coriander, marjoram, mustard seeds, smoked paprika, black pepper, sea salt, and cayenne—and process until fine. Add this mixture to the vital wheat gluten mixture and whisk to combine. Pour in the bouillon mixture and whisk until combined. The dough will be very wet. Knead the dough in the bowl for about 5 minutes, then cover the bowl with a cloth or plastic wrap and let sit for 30 minutes.
- Place a steam basket into a large pot. Add the broth ingredients or water to the pot. Cover and bring to a simmer. Cut 6 sheets of aluminum foil that are about 6 inches wide. Set aside.
- Knead the dough a few times then divide it into 6 equal pieces. Working with one piece at a time, roll and knead it into a hot dog shape that is about 5 inches long. Place it near the bottom of the short side of one piece of aluminum foil and roll the foil over the sausage. You want to leave a little bit of room for the hot dog to expand as it cooks. Now twist the ends—just like a Tootsie Roll wrapper. Proceed with the remaining pieces of dough. When all of the dough has been wrapped, uncover the pot and place the hot dogs around the steam basket. Cover and steam hot dogs for one hour, then turn off the heat and let the hot dogs rest in the pot for another hour.
- At this point, they are ready to serve, but I find the texture gets better if they've had a chance to sit in their foil wrappers in the refrigerator for a day. If you aren't going to use them right away, remove the foil and wrap each hot dog in plastic wrap, place them in a zipper freezer bag and freeze.

Oil-free

RICHA'S RED LENTIL QUINOA CAULIFLOWER STEW

serves 4

Didn't it seem that only a couple of years ago there was no such thing as quinoa? Now you can find red, white, and black quinoa being served in fancy restaurants, added to baked goods, as a rice replacement, and in soups and stews like the one below. What makes quinoa so good? Well, it tastes great—nutty and a bit grassy—but it's also also highly nutritious. One serving of cooked quinoa contains 8 grams of protein and 5 grams of fiber. It's low in fat and contains magnesium, manganese, copper, iron, zinc, and potassium.

2/3 cup dry red lentils (masoor dal), washed and sorted through for stones
1/3 cup quinoa
1/2 cup chopped red onion
1 green chili (remove seeds to adjust heat)
2-inch knob of ginger, peeled
2 cloves of garlic, peeled
2 Tbsp. packed fresh cilantro
1 Tbsp. sesame seeds
1 Tbsp. shredded unsweetened coconut

1/2 tsp. paprika
1/4 tsp. cumin seeds
1/4 tsp. ground cinnamon
1/4 tsp. ground cardamom
1 tsp. coconut oil
1 cup chopped fresh tomato
1 1/2 cups cauliflower, cut into small florets
3/4 tsp. sea salt, or to taste
3 cups water
fresh cilantro and lemon juice for garnish

- ▶ Wash the lentils and quinoa, drain and set aside.
- ▶ In a blender, process the red onion through to the cardamom along with 2 to 3 tablespoons of water, until smooth.
- ▶ Heat a deep pan on medium heat and add the oil. When the oil is hot, add the onion mixture and cook for 7 to 9 minutes or until fragrant and roasted.
- ▶ Add tomato, cauliflower, and salt and stir. Cook for 4 minutes or until tomatoes are softened and juicy. Add the lentils, quinoa, and water. Stir well. Bring to a boil, turn down the heat to simmer and partially cover the pot. Cook for 25 to 30 minutes or until the lentils are tender. Cook longer for thicker consistency. Add more water for thinner stew.
- ▶ Garnish with cilantro, lemon juice and serve hot.

Suggestions

- ▶ To make this oil-free, sauté the onion mixture in water or vegetable broth.

Oliverio

Gluten-free ▲ Oil-free Option ▲ Quick ▲ Easy

Prep time: **15 minutes** *Cook time:* **25 minutes**

SPICY CATSUP

makes 2 cups

Commercially-made catsup contains sugar and high fructose corn syrup, so it's not a product that I stock in my pantry. Catsup is easy to make and it's fun to change up the ingredients to suit your tastes. This one is on the spicy side and gets its sweetness from whole food: dates.

Water or vegetable broth, for sautéing
1 small onion, chopped
1 clove garlic, minced
1 tsp. dried onion flakes
1 tsp. smoked paprika
1/4 tsp. curry powder
1/4 tsp. ground black pepper

Dash red pepper flakes
Dash sea salt
1 (6-ounce) can tomato paste
1/2 cup white vinegar
1/2 cup chopped dates
1/4 cup water
1 tsp. Sriracha

▶ In a small saucepan, warm a generous splash of water or vegetable broth over medium-high heat. Add the onions and garlic and sauté for 5 to 8 minutes, or until soft. Add more water/broth as needed to keep them from sticking.

▶ Stir in the onion flakes, smoked paprika, curry powder, black pepper, red pepper flakes, and sea salt and cook for an additional minute. Add the tomato paste, white vinegar, chopped dates, water, and Sriracha, cover and turn the heat to low. Simmer for 20 minutes.

▶ Let the mixture cool for about 20 minutes, then pour into a blender and process until smooth. Store the catsup in an air-tight container in the refrigerator.

Suggestions
▶ Use your favorite hot sauce in place of the Sriracha.
▶ Use ½ cup of date paste in place of the dates.

Gluten-free ▲ Oil-free ▲ Easy
Total time: **60 minutes**

SMOKY BLACK BEAN, RICE, & VEGGIE BURGERS

serves 4

I like to serve these burgers on a bed of shredded lettuce along with generous amounts of chopped tomatoes, slices of avocado, a lime wedge and several big spoonfuls of Chipotle Cheez Sauce (recipe on page 242), but they're equally tasty on whole wheat or gluten-free buns.

1 cup cooked brown rice
1/4 cup Chipotle Salsa (see recipe on page 245) or store-bought salsa
1/2 Tbsp. cumin
2 tsp. liquid smoke, optional
2 tsp. chile powder
1 tsp. dried thyme
3/4 tsp. smoked paprika
1/2 tsp. dried oregano
1/2 tsp. dried onion flakes

1/2 tsp. ground black pepper
Pinch of sea salt
1 (4-ounce) can diced green chiles
1 small onion, cut into chunks
1 carrot, peeled and cut into chunks
1 stalk celery, cut into chunks
1/2 cup fresh cilantro
1 (15-ounce) can black beans, rinsed and drained
3/4 cup gluten-free rolled oats

— —

▶ In a large bowl, stir together the brown rice, salsa, liquid smoke, cumin, chile powder, thyme, oregano, onion flakes, paprika, black pepper, salt, and green chiles. Set aside.

▶ Add the onion, carrot, and celery to the bowl of a food processor. Pulse until the vegetables are broken down into small pieces. Add the cilantro, black beans, and oats and pulse 2 to 3 times. Add this mixture to the ingredients in the large bowl and stir well to combine thoroughly. Cover bowl and put in the refrigerator for several hours.

▶ Heat a large pan or electric skillet. Spritz lightly with cooking oil. Form 8 patties and carefully place two or three in the pan or skillet. Cook for about 5 minutes or until lightly browned. Very gently turn the burgers and cook for an additional 4 to 5 minutes. Remove them from the pan and cook the remaining burgers.

▶ Serve immediately.

Suggestions

▶ Add splashes of your favorite hot sauce to increase the heat to your liking.

▶ Add ¼ cup fresh or frozen corn kernels when you stir in the green chiles.
▶ Alternatively, bake the burgers at 425 degrees on a parchment-lined baking sheet. Carefully turn the burgers after 20 minutes and bake until browned.

Gluten-free ▲ Oil-free ▲ Easy

Prep time: **20 minutes + 2 hours in refrigerator** *Cook time:* **10 minutes**

Red grapes, sparkling with dew, hanging from the vine.
The bowl of brightly-wrapped candies sitting on the
receptionist's desk, whispering: "Eat me."
A hug from a child.
Any Norman Rockwell painting.
Syrupy, hard-wired, alluring, can't-get-enough.
Sweet.

craving 11
SWEET

ANGELA'S BLUEBERRY "PIT" PIE

serves 6 to 8

In case you are wondering what a "pit" pie is, it's one where some of the interior of the pie is scooped out to make room for sweet blueberry-jamminess—or, as Angela says about spooning out the filling, "This is your treat for having lived through the tantalizing smell while your pie cooked . . . you can now eat the 'pit' of the pie!"

For the jam filling
1 cup water
2 cups fresh blueberries, cleaned and stemmed plus 1 cup for topping the pie
1/4 cup date sugar

For the crust
6 Medjool dates, pitted, chopped
1 cup raw walnuts
4 Tbsp. oat or other flour
1 Tbsp. walnut or coconut oil
2 tsp. date or coconut sugar
Pinch of sea salt

For the pie filling
1 cup non-dairy milk
1 tsp. vanilla
1/3 cup date or coconut sugar, or other dry sweetener
1 tsp. vanilla-flavored liquid stevia
1 tsp. quick rise yeast
1 flax egg (1 Tbsp. ground flaxseed mixed with 2 Tbsp. water)
1 (8-ounce) container of store-bought vegan sour cream
1 tsp. baking powder
1 tsp. cinnamon
Pinch of sea salt

Make the blueberry topping
▶ In a medium-size sauce pan, bring the sugar, water and blueberries to a boil. Reduce the heat to simmer and cook, stirring occasionally, until the sugar and berries have thickened but are still a syrupy consistency. The jam will thicken as it cools so don't overcook. If you don't have it reduced quite enough, it's fine. The syrup will just absorb down into the pie and still be flavorful. Set the pan aside to cool while you make the pie.

Make the crust
▶ Add the nut butter, applesauce, coconut milk or water, stevia, and cinnamon to the processor bowl. Process until very smooth and scrape the mixture into the bowl with the oats. Stir until the mixture is thoroughly combined.

Oliverio

▶ In a food processor, combine the dates, oil, and sugar. Blend until the dates are roughly ground. Add in the walnuts, flour, and salt. Pulse the processor until everything comes together in a loose ball. Press the crust down into the bottom and sides of an 8-inch pie plate. Bake crust at 350 degrees for 10 minutes. Set aside to cool while you make the pie filling.

Make the filling

▶ Warm the nut milk to 110 degrees and add in the yeast, date sugar, flax egg, vanilla and cinnamon. Let mixture sit for about 10 minutes to allow the yeast to grow.

▶ Combine the remaining dry ingredients in a bowl. When the yeast is frothy, pour the liquid into the dry mix and stir to form a batter. The consistency should be similar to cake batter or waffle batter—very airy and thick but easily stirred.

▶ Pour the batter into the crust and bake at 350 degrees for 30 minutes.

▶ Cool the pie and then with a spoon, remove the top layer, about ½ inch worth, from the pie, leaving the outer edge of the pie intact. Pour the warm blueberry jam into the pit area and spread to the edges of the "pit" or center of the pie. Sprinkle the jam topping with the remaining fresh blueberries.

Suggestions

▶ Angela suggests using walnut oil in the crust and walnut milk in the filling of the pie.

▶ This pie is best served warm and/or with a scoop of your favorite vegan vanilla ice cream.

▶ Store in the refrigerator or cover tightly and freeze for longer storage.

▶ This recipe works best with store-bought vegan sour cream rather than the Tofu & Cashew Sour Cream recipe as it has a firmer texture.

Gluten-free

Prep time: **30 minutes** *Cook time:* **30–40 minutes**

BRANDI'S PEANUT BUTTER CHOCOLATE CHIP ESPRESSO BLONDIES

makes 16 squares

Aware of my undying admiration for peanut butter, Brandi created these incredibly soft and fudgy blondies with a hint of coffee and a generous helping of chocolate. To keep myself honest with treats like these, after cooling completely, I cut them into squares, wrap the pieces individually and store in the freezer for when I'm craving something sweet.

1/2 cup plus 2 tablespoons sweet "sticky" white rice flour (not brown rice flour)
1 Tbsp. finely ground espresso or herbal coffee substitute
1/2 tsp. baking powder
1/4 to 1/2 cup mini dairy-free chocolate chips

1 cup creamy roasted natural peanut butter (if you use unsalted peanut butter, add 1/2 teaspoon salt)
1/2 cup unsweetened applesauce
1/2 cup plus 2 Tbsp. pure maple syrup
2 1/2 tsp. pure vanilla extract

▶ Preheat oven to 350 degrees and spray an 8 × 8 aluminum pan with cooking spray.
▶ In a large bowl, add the rice flour, espresso, and baking powder and whisk thoroughly (add salt at this time if needed). Stir in the chocolate chips.
▶ In a separate bowl, add the peanut butter, applesauce, syrup, and vanilla. Stir well with a spoon. Pour over the dry ingredients and stir thoroughly with a spoon until well combined.
▶ Pour the batter (it will be thick) into the prepared pan and smooth out the top and spread out evenly to the edges. Sprinkle extra chocolate chips on top, if desired. Bake 20 to 23 minutes. The edges will have pulled away from the pan and the top should be firm and shiny. A toothpick inserted in the center should come out with a few crumbs on it; it will not be clean. Be careful not to overbake or they won't be fudgy. Let them cool for an hour to firm up before slicing.

Suggestions
▶ Oat flour can be used in place of the white rice flour for tasty results—but the baked blondies will not have the shiny top nor the classic brownie texture.
▶ You can find sticky white rice flour at Asian markets or from Bob's Red Mill.

Gluten-free ▲ Oil-free ▲ Quick ▲ Easy

Total time: **30 minutes**

Sweet

CREAMY RASPBERRY DRESSING

makes 1 cup

When I was a kid, I spent many hours at my friend's house picking sweet red raspberries from the rows and rows of bushes in their garden. Not surprisingly, more berries went into our mouths than made it into our buckets. Though small, raspberries have a whole bunch of nutritional benefits—fiber, vitamins C, E, and K, and other antioxidants that slow the aging process and ease inflammation. This silky dressing isn't going to win any beauty contests, but the flavor more than makes up for its looks.

3-ounces silken tofu
1/2 cup fresh raspberries
1/4 cup water
2 Tbsp. balsamic vinegar

1 small clove garlic
1 tsp. Dijon mustard
1/4 tsp. ground black pepper

▷ Place all ingredients in a high-speed or regular blender and process until smooth.
▷ Store in the refrigerator for up to 1 week.

Suggestions
▷ If you use frozen raspberries, thaw them first.
▷ Try a little horseradish instead of the mustard.
▷ For a slightly sweeter flavor, Dianne of DiannesVeganKitchen.com suggests using white balsamic vinegar.

Gluten-free ▲ Oil-free ▲ Quick ▲ Easy
Total time: **5 minutes**

LAURA'S DATE NUT TRUFFLES

makes about 10

If you're in need of a fuss-free, healthy dessert that will impress guests, look no further. Laura, the "Jazzy Vegetarian," created this simple yet decadent-tasting treat for just such an occasion.

8 large Medjool dates, pitted
1/4 cup raw cashews
3 heaping tablespoons chopped walnuts
2 tablespoons unsweetened shredded
    dried coconut

2 tablespoons unsweetened cacao or
    cocoa powder

▷ Line a small baking sheet with unbleached parchment paper.
▷ Put the dates, cashews, walnuts, and coconut in a high-speed blender and process to the consistency of soft dough. Transfer the date mixture to a medium bowl. Spoon out a heaping tablespoon of the date mixture, and roll it into a ball. Put the cacao or cocoa powder in a small bowl. Roll each truffle in the cocoa powder until coated and place on the prepared sheet.
▷ Refrigerate for 1 hour. Covered tightly and stored in the refrigerator, leftover truffles will keep for about 3 days.

Gluten-free ▲ Oil-free ▲ Quick ▲ Easy

PEANUT JOY SMOOTHIE

serves 2

1 cup brewed chocolate (ground cacao beans), such as Choffy or Crio Brü, chilled

1/2 cup Almond Milk (see recipe on page 35)

2 very ripe bananas, cut into chunks

1/4 cup unsweetened coconut flakes

1/4 cup natural peanut butter

20 drops liquid stevia

1-inch piece turmeric root, peeled or 1/4 tsp. dried

2 cups fresh spinach or kale leaves, chopped

2 to 3 ice cubes

▶ Place all ingredients in a high-speed or regular blender and process until very smooth and creamy.

▶ Serve immediately.

Suggestions

▶ Here's how to brew cacao: place 4 to 5 heaping tablespoons of ground cacao in a French press. Pour about 1½ cups of very hot (nearly boiling, but not quite) water over the grounds and let the mixture sit for 5 minutes. Place the press/top in the carafe and slowly push it down until all of the grounds are compacted. Now pour off the liquid into a glass container and store in the refrigerator until ready to use.

Gluten-free ▲ Oil-free ▲ Easy

Prep time: **4 hours chill time** *Cook time:* **5 minutes**

SUPER SEED DRESSING

makes about 1/3 cup

2 Tbsp. to 1/4 cup white wine vinegar
2 Tbsp. hemp seeds
2 Tbsp. non-dairy milk
1 Tbsp. Date Paste, or to taste (see recipe
    on page 40)

1/2 Tbsp. chia seeds
1/2 Tbsp. white onion, minced
1/2 tsp. Dijon mustard
Pinch sea salt
1 Tbsp. poppy seeds

▷ In a high-speed or regular blender, combine the vinegar, hemp seeds, non-dairy milk, date paste, chia seeds, onion, mustard, and sea salt and process until smooth.
▷ Pour the dressing into a measuring cup or bowl and stir in the poppy seeds. Pour over a giant salad and toss to coat the greens.

Gluten-free ▲ Oil-free ▲ Raw ▲ Quick ▲ Easy
Total time: **less than 10 minutes**

ORANGE CREAMSICLE SANDWICH COOKIES

makes 15 sandwich cookies

Cookies

1/2 cup flaxseed meal
Zest from 1 small orange
1 cup raw macadamia nuts, soaked 8 to 12 hours, rinsed and drained
1/2 cup raw pecans, soaked 8 to 12 hours, rinsed and drained
1/4 cup Date Paste (see recipe on page 40)
1/2 cup fresh orange juice
1/2 tsp. orange-flavored liquid stevia

Filling

3/4 cup raw cashews, soaked 8 to 12 hours, rinsed and drained
1/4 cup unsweetened coconut flakes, soaked about 20 minutes
2 Tbsp. fresh orange juice or nut milk
1/2 tsp. orange-flavored stevia liquid
1/2 tsp. orange zest

Make the cookies

▶ Put the flaxseed meal and the orange zest in a large bowl. Set aside.

▶ In a food processor, pulse the macadamia nuts and the pecans until broken into small pieces. Add the date paste, orange juice and stevia and pulse until everything is combined and the nuts are uniformly in small bits. Do not process so much that you end up with nut butter!

▶ Pour this mixture into the flaxseed meal and stir to thoroughly combine. Scrape onto a non-stick dehydrator sheet and spread and pat down until it is about ¼ inch thick. Using a 2-inch round cookie cutter, press into the dough until you have about 30 circles. The idea is to make indents; you won't be moving the cookies until later.

▶ Put the tray in the dehydrator and set it to 115 degrees. Dehydrate for 2 to 3 hours, then remove the tray. Using the 2-inch cookie cutter again, press down into the indents you already made so that you go all the way through the dough. Carefully transfer the rounds to another dehydrator tray—this time one lined with a mesh sheet. You will have scraps of dough; transfer those to a tray lined with a mesh sheet. Place both trays back into the dehydrator and dry for another 12 to 24 hours, depending on how crisp you want the cookies to be. Check periodically until the texture is just right.

▶ When crisp, store the cookies in an air-tight container until ready to assemble the sandwich cookies. Reserve the "scraps" and use to crumble on top of ice cream or your morning oatmeal.

Make the filling

▶ Put all of the ingredients in a high-speed or regular blender and process until smooth. You will need to scrape down the sides occasionally. This won't get perfectly smooth; you will see some texture from the coconut flakes.

Assemble the sandwich cookies

▶ Divide the filling between fifteen cookies. Top each cookie with one of the remaining cookies and gently press down. Place the cookies on a small baking sheet that's been lined with wax or parchment paper. Cover and store in the refrigerator.

Suggestions

▶ These sandwich cookies would be out-of-this-world dipped in melted chocolate (à la Mystical Mint Cookies on pages 102 and 103); add ½ teaspoon of pure orange extract to the melted chocolate.

Gluten-free ▲ Oil-free ▲ Raw
Total time: **22 hours, including soaking and dehydrating time**

RASPBERRY CANNOLI TARTLETS

makes 6

There is a large Italian population in my hometown of Cleveland with several Italian delis and bakeries scattered throughout the region. Among other sweets and treats, cannoli were a big part of my childhood and we were particular about them. Our ultimate test of an Italian bakery was whether or not they filled the crispy cannoli shells on order, rather than passing off pre-filled (and therefore soggy) pastries. I especially liked cannoli that had a thin chocolate layer on the inside of the shell so I've recreated that here with my high raw version of this famous Italian pastry.

I use a 3½-inch large muffin pan for this recipe, but you could use a regular muffin tin as well—you'll just get more, though smaller tartlets.

Crust
1 1/2 cups raw walnuts
3/4 cup pitted, chopped Medjool dates
1 1/2 tsp. anise seed
2 Tbsp. water
2 tsp. vanilla extract
1 tsp. maca powder, optional

Chocolate layer
1/2 cup vegan stevia-sweetened semi-sweet chocolate chips

Raspberry filling
12-ounces frozen raspberries
4 Tbsp. water
2 Tbsp. kuzu powder
1 Tbsp. fresh orange juice

1/2 tsp. stevia powder, or your favorite sweetener, to taste

Ricotta topping
1 cup raw cashews, soaked for a few hours, rinsed and drained
1/4 cup plain, non-dairy yogurt (I prefer soy yogurt here as it is a little more tart than almond yogurt)
1/4 cup plus 1 Tbsp. water
2 tsp. fresh lemon juice
1 tsp. nutritional yeast
Pinch citric acid, optional
Cacao nibs, for topping, optional
Chopped pistachios, for topping, optional
Fresh raspberries, for topping, optional

Make the crust

▶ Place six 3½-inch muffin liners in a 6-muffin tin. Set aside.

▶ In the bowl of a food processor, add the walnuts, dates, and anise seed and process until chunky. Add the water, vanilla extract, and maca powder and process until the dough forms a ball. Divide the mixture between the 6 muffins liners. Using your fingers, press the dough down along the bottom of each tin. No need to try to go up the sides—you just want to make sure the bottoms are evenly covered. Set aside.

Make the chocolate layer

▶ In a small saucepan or in a microwave-safe glass bowl, gently melt the chocolate chips. When completely melted, divide the chocolate between the muffin cups and spread the chocolate over the crust. Again, no need to try and be perfect here, you just want to get a fairly even layer of chocolate on top of the crust. Place the muffin tin in the freezer or refrigerator while you prepare the raspberry layer.

Make the raspberry layer

▶ Whisk together the water, kuzu, and stevia powder in a small measuring cup. Set aside.

▶ In a small saucepan, heat the raspberries over medium-high heat, stirring occasionally. When they begin to soften and break down, add the kuzu mixture. This will whiten the mixture, but only for a minute or two. Stir until the raspberries begin to thicken and the white color clears. Stir in the orange juice and adjust for sweetness.

▶ Remove the tartlets from the freezer or refrigerator and divide the raspberry mixture between the tins. Spread so you have an even layer and tap the tin on the counter a few times. Put the muffin tin back in the refrigerator while you prepare the ricotta layer.

Make the ricotta layer

▶ In a high-speed or regular blender, combine all of the ricotta ingredients and process until very smooth. You will need to tamp the mixture and/or scrape down the sides a few times. Taste and adjust for tartness and sweetness.

▶ Remove the tartlets from the refrigerator and divide the ricotta mixture between them, smoothing the ricotta so that it completely covers the tartlets. Sprinkle on cacao nibs and pistachios, if using, and top each tart with a couple of raspberries, if desired. Return the tartlets to the refrigerator for an hour or two to firm up.

Suggestions

▶ Raspberry sweetness varies, so be sure and taste the raspberry mixture before dividing it between the tartlets.

▶ The ricotta is sweet enough for my tastes without adding any additional sweetener but feel free to adjust the taste to your preferences.

Gluten-free ▲ High Raw ▲ Oil-free

Total time: **1 hour 30 minutes**

The morning sun in your eyes when
you forget to close the blinds.
The candy lemon drops Aunt Phyllis slipped
you when your mom wasn't looking.
A slice of rhubarb pie.
Tingly, tangy, mouth-puckering, eye-opening.
Tart.

craving 12
TART

CHERRY-POMEGRANATE REFRIGERATOR JAM

makes 1 pint

There's nothing like spreading a little fiber, vitamins C, K, and B, calcium, melatonin, calcium, and potassium on your morning toast!

1 1/2 cups frozen sweet cherries
1 cup 100% pomegranate juice
1/4 cup chia seeds

1/2 tsp. fresh lemon juice
1/2 tsp. cherry-flavored liquid stevia
1/4 tsp. vanilla-flavored liquid stevia

▶ Put the cherries and the pomegranate juice in a small saucepan and bring to a boil. Turn the heat down and simmer the cherries for 15 to 20 minutes.
▶ Remove the cherry mixture from the heat and stir in the chia seeds, lemon juice, and stevia liquids. Allow the mixture to cool for a while before spooning into a pint-sized mason jar.
▶ Store in the refrigerator for up to 1 week.

Suggestions
▶ Use your favorite berry in place of the cherries.
▶ Use your preferred sweetener to taste.
▶ Use 2 tsp. kuzu powder in place of the chia seeds. Combine the powder with 4 tsp. water, and whisk into the cherry-pomegranate mixture during the last 2 to 3 minutes of cooking.

Gluten-free ▲ Oil-free ▲ Quick ▲ Easy
Prep time: **5 minutes** *Cook time:* **15-20 minutes**

CHOCOLATE-COATED KEY LIME COCONUT CREAM PIE

serves 8

Key limes are the cutest citrus fruits on the planet! I'm always happy to see them appear each year in my grocery store. This creamy, tart pie is a treat on a warm day, and the zing from the lime juice pairs nicely with the sweet chocolate.

1 recipe Raw Pie Crust (see page 59 for recipe)

Chocolate coating

1 cup stevia-sweetened semi-sweet chocolate chips
1 Tbsp. virgin coconut oil
1/2 tsp. vanilla extract

Filling

1 cup full-fat coconut milk
1/3 cup coconut butter, softened (page 37)
12.3-ounces extra-firm silken tofu
1 Tbsp. key lime zest
1/4 cup key lime juice (about 10)
1/2 tsp. liquid stevia, or to taste

▷ Place the chocolate and coconut oil in a double boiler and gently melt. Remove from the heat and stir in the vanilla extract. Pour about ⅔ of the chocolate onto the bottom of the crust. Smooth the chocolate all along the bottom and up along the sides. It doesn't have to be perfect—you won't see it (but you will taste it)! Place the pie pan in the refrigerator while you prepare the filling.

▷ In a high-speed or regular blender, combine all of the filling ingredients and process until silky smooth. Taste and adjust the sweetness. Remove the pie pan from the refrigerator and pour in the filling. Shake the pan gently a few times to evenly distribute the filling and to remove any air pockets.

▷ Gently reheat that little bit of chocolate remaining and drizzle it over the top of the filling. Place the pie in the refrigerator for several hours to set.

Suggestions

▷ Key limes not in season? Substitute with fresh lime juice.
▷ Silken tofu brands differ in consistency, flavor, and how they perform in recipes. My preference is Mori-Nu which has a mild flavor and sets better than other brands I've tried.
▷ The chocolate on the bottom and top gets very firm, so use a sharp knife when slicing the pie.

Gluten-free

Prep time: **20 minutes** *Chill time:* **4-5 hours**

EASY PICKLED SLAW

makes about 4 cups

This recipe is a take on curtido, a Salvadoran slaw recipe. This is yummy alongside Somer's Tempeh Tacos on page 213 or atop the Jackfruit & Pinto Bean Tostadas on page 302.

2 cups water
1 1/2 cups apple cider vinegar
1 tsp. dried oregano
1/2 tsp. cumin
1/4 tsp. ground coriander
Pinch red pepper flakes
5 to 6 peppercorns
2 cups shredded green cabbage

2 carrots, peeled and shredded or grated
1 parsnip, peeled and shredded or grated
1/2 medium-sized onion, thinly sliced
1 small red bell pepper, seeded, cut in
    half and thinly sliced
1/4 cup chopped pickled pepperoncini
    or banana peppers
1 tsp. pure maple syrup

▶ In a saucepan, bring the water, apple cider vinegar, oregano, cumin, coriander, red pepper flakes, and peppercorn to a boil. Remove the saucepan from the heat, cover, and set aside while you prepare the rest of the ingredients.

▶ In a large bowl, toss together the cabbage, carrots, parsnip, onion, and bell pepper. Pour the water-apple cider mixture over the vegetables, toss and cover bowl with a large plate. Let sit for 3 minutes, stir, and cover again. Let sit another 3 minutes.

▶ Thoroughly drain the cabbage mixture (discarding the liquid). Return the slaw to the large bowl and add the pepperoncini and maple syrup. Stir well. Cover the slaw and refrigerate for at least 2 hours before serving.

Gluten-free ▲ Oil-free ▲ Quick ▲ Easy

LEMON-COCONUT SPIRULINA BALLS

makes about 20

Normally one should run screaming from food that is this green—but these bite-sized treats won't hurt you! Spirulina is a blue-green algae that is rich in iron, chlorophyll, beta carotene, and other nutrients. If you are put off by the slight seaweed smell and taste of spirulina, just omit it—but the lemon and coconut really do mask the flavor.

1 cup raw pecan pieces	2 Tbsp. fresh lemon juice
1 cup chopped dates	2 Tbsp. coconut milk
1/2 cup unsweetened raw coconut flakes	1 Tbsp. spirulina
2 Tbsp. hemp seeds	

▶ Put the pecans and dates into the bowl of a food processor and pulse until broken down into small pieces. Add the remaining ingredients and process until smooth. You will need to scrape down the sides of the bowl a few times. The mixture will form a ball.

▶ Scrape the mixture into a bowl, cover with plastic wrap and refrigerate for an hour or two. Using a small spoon, scoop up about 1 heaping teaspoon of the mixture and roll into a ball. Place in an air-tight container. Continue with the rest of the mixture. Store the balls in the refrigerator.

Suggestions

▶ If you don't have spirulina, you could use a green protein powder (which often contain spirulina), or just make the balls without it.

Gluten-free ▲ Oil-free ▲ Raw ▲ Quick ▲ Easy

Total time: **2 hours, including chill time**

PAULIE'S SLAW

serves 4

My friend Paul sent me an email a while back with only eleven words in it—all of them the ingredients to a salad he'd made that he thought I might like for its unusual tastiness and powerful nutritional benefits. As usual, Paul was right. I tinkered with those eleven words and came up with my version of Paulie's slaw.

1/4 of a small head of purple cabbage, thinly sliced
1/4 cup Vidalia onion, chopped
2 stalks celery, chopped
1 cup broccoli, chopped into small pieces

1 small red grapefruit, peeled and chopped into small pieces
Zest of 1 lemon
Zest of 1 lime
Splash of white wine or sherry vinegar
Pinch ground black pepper

▶ Combine all of the ingredients in a bowl and stir to combine.
▶ Serve immediately or store in an air-tight container in the refrigerator.

Suggestions
▶ Soak the chopped onion in cool water for about 15 minutes, then drain. This will take some of the edge off of it.
▶ This slaw gets softer and less crunchy over time.

Gluten-free ▲ Oil-free ▲ Raw ▲ Quick ▲ Easy
Total time: **10 minutes**

LEMON-GARLIC BAKED TOFU

serves 4

I make a version of this baked tofu at least once a week. The beauty of this method is that you can change up the flavors by subbing with different spices and herbs. Keep the vegetable broth and tamari—but use cumin, chile powder, and some chipotle in adobo for a spicy, Mexican-inspired version.

1/2 cup Vegetable Broth (see recipe on page 60) or store-bought low-sodium broth
1/4 cup fresh lemon juice
1/4 cup low-sodium tamari or liquid aminos

Zest of 1 lemon
1 tsp. ground black pepper
1 tsp. garlic powder
12-ounces extra-firm tofu, pressed

▶ Preheat oven to 425 degrees.
▶ In a small baking pan, whisk together the vegetable broth, lemon juice, tamari, lemon zest, pepper, and garlic powder.
▶ Cut the tofu into large pieces, strips, or cubes, as directed on pages 30 and 31. Place in the marinade and turn to coat thoroughly. Let the pieces marinate for 30 minutes, turning occasionally. Bake the tofu, turning once or twice, for 45 to 60 minutes or until browned. Add a splash of vegetable broth or water if the pan dries out before the tofu is browned.

Suggestions
▶ Use the large pieces of tofu as a sandwich filling; the strips fit nicely into pita breads or inside of tortillas.
▶ Sprinkle cubes on top of a big, fresh salad.
▶ Replace the lemon zest and lemon juice with lime zest and lime juice and add the baked tofu to the Raw/Not Raw Vegetable Barley Bowl (see recipe on page 196).

Gluten-free ▲ Oil-free ▲ Easy
Total time: **60 minutes**

Tart

MEYER LEMON & LIME PARFAITS WITH DATE-NUT CRUNCH

makes 4

This dessert would fit happily in the Sweet chapter, but the sweetness in this parfait plays only a subtle supporting role to the pop of the citrus. Regular lemons work just fine if you can't find Meyer lemons, but you may need to adjust the sweetness.

Pudding

1 1/2 cups raw cashew pieces, soaked 8 to 12 hours, rinsed and drained
7 Medjool dates, soaked for a few hours and drained
1/2 cup canned full-fat coconut milk
1/2 cup fresh Meyer lemon juice (about 2)
1/4 cup fresh lime juice (about 2)
1 large ripe banana
1 Tbsp. pure maple syrup
Zest of 2 Meyer lemons
Zest of 1 lime
1/4 tsp. vanilla extract

Date-Nut Crunch

1 cup pecans
1/4 cup pumpkin or sunflower seeds
3 Medjool dates, roughly chopped
1/2 cup toasted rice cereal
1 Tbsp. pure maple syrup
1 Tbsp. sesame seeds
1 tsp. cinnamon
1/2 tsp. vanilla extract
Zest of 1 orange

▶ In a blender, combine the cashews, dates, coconut milk, lemon and lime juices, banana, maple syrup, lemon and lime zest, and vanilla extract. Process until very smooth. Taste and adjust the sweetness and tartness. Set aside.

▶ Heat a small pan over medium-low heat. Gently toast the pecans, pumpkin, or sunflower seeds. Remove from the heat. In a food processor, pulse the toasted nuts and dates a few times to break them into small pieces. Add the toasted rice cereal and pulse a couple more times. Pour the mixture into a medium-sized bowl and stir in the maple syrup, sesame seeds, cinnamon, vanilla extract and orange zest. Remove ½ cup of the date-nut mixture and set aside.

▶ Put one heaping tablespoon of the date-nut mixture at the bottom of 4 small or tall glasses. Divide half (about 1½ cups) of the lemon-lime pudding between the four bowls/glasses. Top with the remaining date-nut mixture (not the reserved portion) between the four bowls/glasses. Divide the remaining pudding between the bowls/glasses and top with the reserved ½ cup of date-nut mixture. Cover and chill for several hours before serving.

Suggestions

▶ Substitute regular lemon for Meyer lemon.
▶ Use agave nectar or stevia instead of maple syrup in the pudding.
▶ Substitute walnuts for pecans.
▶ To make this 100% raw, use raw nuts and don't toast them (in the Date-Nut Crunch), and use agave nectar in place of the maple syrup.

Gluten-free ▲ High Raw
Oil-free ▲ Easy

The smell of cinnamon. Steam rising from a mug of chamomile tea.
Your favorite sweater worn at the elbows and soft as clouds.
Your Labradoodle leaning against your legs.
Comforting, homey, toasty, soothing. Warm.

craving 13
WARM

5-WAY CHILI

serves 4

When I was a poor (yet always famished) 20-something, I lived in Cincinnati, Ohio and worked downtown for a commercial photographer. His studio wasn't far from a Skyline Chili restaurant, and when I was feeling flush with cash, I'd treat myself to a couple of hot dogs smothered in their famous chili and topped with onions and a big, fluffy pile of cheddar cheese. I always vaguely regretted my indulgence, but soon enough, I was craving those dogs again.

5-way refers to the number of different toppings one can add to their Skyline chili: kidney beans, chopped onions, spaghetti, and cheese (the chili counts as 1 way). My version substitutes green lentils for the ground beef in the original. Like most soups and stews, this tastes even better the next day, so try to make it ahead.

2/3 cup green or brown lentils, sorted through and rinsed (about 1 1/2 cups cooked)

1 large onion, peeled and chopped

2 cloves garlic, peeled and minced

2 large carrots, peeled and chopped

Water or vegetable broth for sautéing

1/2 Tbsp. chili powder

1/4 tsp. ground cinnamon

1/2 Tbsp. smoked paprika

1 tsp. ground cumin

1 tsp. dried onion flakes

1/4 tsp. ground allspice

1/4 tsp. ground coriander

1 cup unsweetened apple juice or water

1 (28-ounce) can crushed tomatoes

2 (15-ounce) cans kidney beans, drained and rinsed

1 bay leaf

1 Tbsp. cacao or cocoa powder

1/2 Tbsp. vegan Worcestershire sauce

1/2 Tbsp. apple cider vinegar

2 Tbsp. Date Paste (see recipe on page 40)

Sea salt and ground black pepper, to taste, optional

Chopped onions, for topping

Grated Cheddar Cheez, for topping (see page 227 for recipe), or store-bought vegan cheese

Raw zucchini cut into spirals, for topping, optional

- Put the lentils in a small sauce pan, cover with water and bring it to a boil. Turn down the heat to a low simmer and cook for about 20 minutes, or until the lentils are tender. Add more water as they are cooking, if needed. Drain the lentils and set aside.
- Meanwhile, in a large pot, sauté the onion, garlic, and carrot in water or vegetable broth for about 5 minutes.
- Stir in the chili powder through the cinnamon and cook for another minute. Add the apple juice or water, diced tomatoes, kidney beans, lentils, and bay leaf and cook, uncovered, for 10 minutes.
- Add the cacao or cocoa powder, Worcestershire sauce, apple cider vinegar, and date paste. Cover and simmer for an additional 30 minutes, stirring occasionally.
- Remove the bay leaf and divide the chili between four bowls and top with onion, Cheddar Cheez, and zucchini "noodles."

Suggestions
- Use pinto beans in place of kidney beans.
- If you don't like lentils, try substituting with about 1 cup cooked oat groats or ½ cup uncooked, gluten-free rolled oats. Stir in the oats when you add the tomatoes.
- Go for a 6-way and add chopped fresh tomatoes.
- For added richness, my friend Somer suggests stirring in a heaping tablespoon of almond butter towards the end of cooking time.
- This tastes great on top of brown rice linguini or fettucine noodles.
- Sprinkle crumbled Tempeh Bacon (see recipe on page 63) on top.

Gluten-free ▲ Oil-free ▲ Easy
Prep time: **15 minutes** *Cook time:* **35–40 minutes**

BECKY'S GINGERED COCONUT–SWEET POTATO SOUP

serves 2 to 3

This is a simple one-pot soup that's perfect on a chilly evening. The puréed sweet potatoes and rich coconut milk make this warming, gingery dish stick-to-your-ribs satisfying! Serve up big bowls with crusty bread for dipping and call it a day or dish this out as a starter to a hearty meal.

1 cup red onion, diced
2 Tbsp. toasted sesame or walnut oil
2 sweet potatoes, cut into bite-sized
    cubes
2 cups water

2 cloves minced garlic
2 Tbsp. minced fresh ginger
2 Tbsp. miso paste
1 (13.5-ounce) can of coconut milk
Cashews, for garnish

▶ Sauté the onions in the oil until they start to brown, then add the sweet potatoes, water, garlic, and ginger. Bring to a boil, then cover and simmer until the potatoes are tender, about 20 minutes.
▶ Put ½ cup of broth from the soup in a glass measuring cup or small bowl and whisk in the miso. Stir until completely dissolved and pour back into the soup. Add the coconut milk, then either transfer the soup to a blender or use an immersion blender to purée.
▶ Simmer for 5 more minutes, and serve topped with a handful of cashews.

Suggestions
▶ To make this oil-free, sauté the onions in vegetable broth or water.

Gluten-free ▲ Oil-free Option ▲ Quick ▲ Easy
Total time: **40–45 minutes**

Warm

BLACK & BLUE CRUMBLE WITH VANILLA ICE CREAM

serves 4

This dessert is the essence of summer, though thanks to frozen berries which are available year-round, you don't have to wait until the temperature rises.

Naturally sweet but low in calories, blackberries are packed with fiber, antioxidants, vitamin C, vitamin K, folic acid and manganese.

2 cups fresh or frozen blackberries
2 cups fresh or frozen blueberries
1/2 tsp. cinnamon
1/4 cup Date Paste (see recipe on page 40), or to taste
2 tsp. kuzu powder

3 tsp. cool water
1/2 tsp. vanilla extract
1 cup High Raw Blueberry Granola (see recipe on page 178)
1 batch Vanilla Ice Cream (see recipe on page 159)

▷ In a small saucepan, bring the berries, date paste, and cinnamon to a simmer. Cook for about 10 minutes, stirring occasionally.
▷ Meanwhile, whisk the kuzu powder and water together and set aside. When the berries have started to break down, stir in the kuzu/water mixture and stir until thickened, 2 to 3 minutes. Remove from the heat and stir in the vanilla extract.
▷ Divide mixture between three small bowls. Top with High Raw Blueberry Granola and Vanilla Ice Cream.

Suggestions
▷ Instead of blackberries and blueberries, try this with peaches, raspberries, cooked apples or your favorite fruit.

Gluten-free ▲ Oil-free ▲ Easy
Total time: **40–45 minutes**

CAPONATA

makes about 3 cups

I come from a family of pre-dinner snackers. On the one hand it was great because it was a way to wind down from a busy day, to socialize, and of course, what's not to like about eating? The downside is that more often than not, by the time dinner came around, no one was really hungry! Caponata was one of the regularly featured appetizers at family snack time, and appropriately so, since my dad's mom, Annunciata, a.k.a. Lillian, hailed from Sicily, where caponata originated. For a different taste, use balsamic vinegar in place of the red wine vinegar and top with toasted pine nuts.

Water or vegetable broth for sautéing
1 to 1 1/2 pound eggplant, peeled and
    cut into 1/2-inch cubes
1 medium zucchini, cut into 1/2-inch
    cubes
1 medium onion, chopped
4 cloves garlic, roughly chopped
1 cup chopped tomatoes

2 Tbsp. capers, drained
3 Tbsp. red wine vinegar
1/4 cup sliced green olives
1/4 cup chopped roasted red peppers
1/2 tsp. dried basil
1/2 tsp. dried oregano
1/3 cup fresh basil, chopped
1/2 tsp. ground black pepper

▶ In a large, deep skillet heat the water or broth over medium-high heat and add the eggplant, zucchini, onion, and garlic. Sauté until eggplant becomes soft, 10 to 15 minutes. Add the tomatoes, capers, red wine vinegar, olives, roasted red peppers, spices, and black pepper. Turn down the heat to medium-low, cover, and simmer for 10 to 12 minutes. The vegetables should be very soft.

▶ Let the caponata cool a little bit, then stir in the fresh basil. Serve immediately, or cover and store in the refrigerator. Before serving, let the caponata come to room temperature.

Suggestions
▶ Of course this is delicious on crusty bread or crisp crackers, but it makes a mighty-fine sandwich or pita filling, too.

Gluten-free ▲ Oil-free ▲ Easy
Total time: **40–45 minutes**

Warm

CARROT-GINGER-TURMERIC STEAMER

serves 2

I think of this as my anti-cancer drink because ginger, turmeric, and carrots all bring their own powerful properties to attacking rogue cells—especially in certain types of cancer such as melanoma, lung, stomach, bladder, colon, and prostate cancers.

4-inch piece of ginger root
4-inch piece of turmeric root
2 small carrots

2 cups coconut milk
10 to 12 drops of vanilla-flavored liquid
  stevia

— —

▶ Juice the ginger root, turmeric root, and carrots. Combine the juice with the coconut milk and the stevia. Heat gently on the stove or in a microwave. This is best warm rather than hot. Serve immediately.

Suggestions

▶ Coconut milk brands vary widely in flavor. I prefer a brand with a strong coconut taste, but use your favorite, or use another non-dairy milk.

▶ Go raw and drink this cold.

▶ An easier method if you don't have a juicer:

  1/2 cup bottled carrot juice (make sure it's 100% carrot juice)
  2 cups coconut milk
  1/2 tsp. ground ginger
  1/4 tsp. ground turmeric
  10 to 12 drops vanilla-flavored stevia liquid

  Whisk together and enjoy.

Gluten-free ▲ Oil-free ▲ Raw Option ▲ Quick ▲ Easy

Total time: **10 minutes**

TOMATO-POTATO BRUSCHETTA

serves 4

I love snacky meals—lots of small bites and bits of different things. Pair this with Roasted Garlic & Fresh Herb Cream Cheez, the Zucchini, Apricot & Almond Salad, and the Salty & Sweet Marinated Mushrooms for a nice little spread of tapas.

1 cup Vegetable Broth (see page 60 for recipe) or store-bought low-sodium vegetable broth
1 large potato, peeled and cut into bite-sized cubes
1 small onion, finely chopped
1 tsp. dried thyme
1/2 tsp. sweet paprika

Pinch ground black pepper
2 cups cherry tomatoes
2 cloves garlic, roughly chopped
Fresh basil, cut into strips, for garnish
8 pieces Raw Pesto Crackers (see recipe on page 182) or 8 slices whole-grain crusty bread

----

▶ Preheat the oven to 425 degrees. In a small baking dish, combine the broth, potatoes, onion, thyme, paprika, and black pepper and bake for about 30 minutes, stirring occasionally. The potatoes should be soft and most of the liquid absorbed.
▶ Stir in the cherry tomatoes and the garlic and bake for an additional 10 to 15 minutes, or until the tomatoes just start to split. Remove from the oven and let cool slightly.
▶ Place two pieces each of Raw Pesto Crackers or bread onto four plates. Divide the tomato-potato mixture and spoon on top of the crackers/bread slices. Sprinkle fresh basil on top.

Suggestions
▶ Sliced kalamata olives would be superb sprinkled on top with the basil.

Gluten-free ▲ Oil-free ▲ Easy

GINGER-MINT TONIC

makes 3 cups

Whenever that scratchy feeling in my throat signals the onset of a cold, I brew up this simple tonic. It's powerful stuff. I usually drink mine without sweetener, but add your favorite to taste, if you like.

4 cups water
1/2 cup pieces of fresh ginger, unpeeled
1 cup loosely-packed fresh mint leaves

4 2-inch pieces of orange peel
5 to 10 drops liquid stevia, to taste, or your
    favorite sweetener to taste, optional

▶ In a medium-sized saucepan, bring the water, ginger, mint, and orange peel to a boil. Turn down the heat and simmer for 2 minutes. Turn off the heat, cover the pan and let the mixture steep for 30 minutes.

▶ Strain the mixture through a sieve, discarding the solids, and either use the tonic immediately or store in an air-tight container in the refrigerator.

Gluten-free ▲ Oil-free ▲ Quick ▲ Easy
Total time: **35 minutes**

JACKFRUIT & PINTO BEAN TOSTADAS

serves 4 to 6

1 (20- or 24-ounce) bottle or can of
    young jackfruit (in water or brine),
    rinsed and drained
1 small onion, chopped
2 cloves garlic, minced
1 (15-ounce) can pinto beans, rinsed and
    drained
1 tsp. cumin
1 tsp. dried onion flakes
1 tsp. garlic powder
1 tsp. chile powder
1 tsp. dried oregano
1 tsp. ground black pepper
1 tsp. liquid smoke, optional
1/4 tsp. smoked paprika
1 tsp. pure maple syrup

1 cup canned crushed tomatoes
1/2 cup Vegetable Broth (see recipe
    on page 60), or store-bought low
    sodium vegetable broth
8 Raw Corn Tortillas (see recipe on page
    46) or store-bought gluten-free or
    whole wheat tortillas
Chopped red or green cabbage
Chopped lettuce
Diced red onion
Diced tomatoes
Chopped cilantro
Chopped avocado
Tofu & Cashew Sour Cream (see recipe
    on page 61), or store-bought vegan
    sour cream

▶ Roughly chop the jackfruit.

▶ In a large sauce pan, sauté the onions and garlic in water or broth over medium-high heat until soft, about 5 minutes. Add the jackfruit and cook, stirring occasionally, until the edges begin to brown. Add the pinto beans and a splash of water or broth to scrape up the browned bits.

▶ Stir in the cumin, dried onion flakes, garlic powder, chile powder, oregano, black pepper, liquid smoke, and smoked paprika. Cook for 1 minute then stir in the maple syrup, tomatoes and vegetable broth. Let the mixture come to a boil, then turn down the heat to low, cover and simmer for about 30 minutes, stirring now and then until the mixture thickens. If the mixture gets too dry, add some more vegetable broth or water.

▶ Divide the jackfruit mixture between 8 tortillas and garnish with cabbage, lettuce, onion, etc.

Gluten-free ▲ Oil-free ▲ Easy

Prep time: **10 minutes** *Cook time:* **30–45 minutes**

Oliverio

ROASTED VEGETABLE TERRINE WITH LEMON-THYME SAUCE

serves 4 to 6

I'm just going to be straight-up about it. This is slow-food. It's the kind of dish you make for a special occasion or on a lazy Sunday. But—and you knew that was coming, didn't you—if you break it down into parts, you can divide up the work: roast the vegetables one day; make the lemon-thyme sauce on another. The reward is a visually stunning, gastronomically delicious main course—and because it can be eaten at room temperature—it's ideal for a buffet lunch, brunch, or a picnic.

Terrine

1 red bell pepper, stemmed, seeded and cut in half

1 orange or yellow bell pepper, stemmed, seeded and cut in half

1 (1-pound) eggplant, peeled and cut into 1/2-inch thick rounds

1 medium-sized zucchini, cut in half widthwise and then into 1/4-inch planks lengthwise

1 medium-sized yellow squash cut in half widthwise and then into 1/4-inch planks lengthwise

1 large onion, peeled and cut into 1/2-inch thick half moons

2 medium-sized potatoes, peeled and cut into bite-sized pieces

2 cloves garlic, peeled and smashed

1/2 cup non-dairy milk

2 Tbsp. nutritional yeast

1 Tbsp. Parmesan Cheez (see recipe on page 54) or store-bought vegan Parmesan cheese substitute

2 tsp. fresh lemon juice

1/2 tsp. garlic powder

1/4 tsp. smoked paprika

Pinch turmeric powder

Pinch sea salt and ground black pepper

3 to 4 large fresh parsley leaves, left whole, to decorate the top of the terrine

Lemon-Thyme Sauce

1 cup Vegetable Broth (see page 60 for recipe) or store-bought low-sodium vegetable broth

1/4 cup raw cashew pieces

Zest of 1 lemon

2 Tbsp. fresh lemon juice

1 small clove garlic

Pinch black pepper

1/2 tsp. fresh thyme

Make the terrine

▶ Preheat the broiler to 500 degrees and place the bell pepper halves on a baking sheet that's been lined with aluminum foil. Broil the peppers until the skins have blackened. Place the peppers in a paper bag, close the top, and let rest for about 15 minutes. Take the peppers out of the bag and let cool enough so that you can handle them. Carefully remove the skins without breaking up the peppers. You want them to say in big pieces so that you can create layers in the terrine. Set aside.

▶ While the peppers broil, place the eggplant slices in a colander, sprinkle with salt, and let sit for 15–20 minutes. Rinse thoroughly and pat dry. Set aside.

▶ Preheat the oven to 400 degrees. Lightly spray a baking sheet with cooking oil and place the eggplant slices, zucchini and yellow squash planks, and onion on the pan in one layer—you may need 2 pans. Lightly spritz the vegetables with oil and bake for 45–60 minutes, turning once. The vegetables should be very soft and lightly browned. Remove from the oven and let cool.

▶ While the vegetables are cooking, make the mashed potatoes. Fill a medium-sized pot with water and bring to a boil. Add the potatoes and the smashed garlic, turn the heat to medium-low and cook until tender, about 15 minutes. Drain and set aside. In a medium-sized bowl, stir together the nutritional yeast, Parmesan Cheez, lemon juice, garlic powder, smoked paprika, turmeric, and salt and pepper. Add the mashed potatoes and the non-dairy milk and using a potato masher, cream the potatoes until there are no lumps. Taste and adjust the seasonings.

▶ To assemble the terrine, line a 9 × 5 loaf pan with plastic wrap. Place the parsley leaves at the bottom of the pan. Place the red peppers over the parsley, covering as much of the bottom of the pan as you can. No need for every nook and cranny to be covered, however. Scooping out ½ of the mashed potatoes, carefully spread and press them onto the red peppers, going to the sides and corners. Press the potatoes down firmly. This is the adhesive layer—it's going to keep everything together!

▶ Now layer on the zucchini and yellow squash, then the onions, and then the yellow bell pepper. Layer the remaining half of the mashed potatoes over the bell pepper, pressing down again to reach the sides and corners of the loaf pan. Lastly, layer on the eggplant slices, pressing them into the potatoes.

▶ Bring the plastic wrap up and over to cover the top (which will be the bottom when unmolded) of the terrine. Add another layer of wrap if there are any uncovered spots. Place the terrine in the refrigerator and place some weight on top, such as a couple of 15-ounce cans. Let the terrine rest in the refrigerator overnight.

Make the sauce

▶ When ready to serve the terrine, prepare the sauce. Combine everything but the fresh thyme in a high-speed or regular blender. Process until very smooth—it may take a minute or more.

▶ Pour the sauce into a small pot and add the thyme. Heat over medium-high heat until bubbly, then turn down the heat to medium-low and stir often. The sauce will thicken slightly and continue to thicken as it cools. Let the sauce cool a bit before using it with the terrine.

Warm

305

Serve the terrine

▶ Remove the terrine from the refrigerator an hour or so before serving. Peel back the top layer of plastic wrap and place a flat plate on top of the loaf pan. Carefully invert the pan and tap a few times to get the terrine to pop out onto the plate. Gently remove all of the plastic wrap.

▶ To serve, slice the terrine and ladle on a couple of tablespoons of sauce.

Gluten-free ▲ Oil-free ▲ Easy

TRACEY'S ROASTED VEGGIES IN PHYLLO PILLOWS

makes 6

1 pound carrots, peeled and sliced into matchsticks
1 head broccoli, chopped into bite sized pieces
2 tsp. sea salt, divided
1 tsp. ground black pepper, divided
refined coconut oil, for roasting the vegetables
1 package vegan phyllo dough, thawed

1/4 cup coconut oil, plus an additional 2 Tbsp., melted

Tools required:
Pastry brush
Plastic wrap
Damp kitchen towel
Baking sheet

▶ Preheat oven to 375 degrees. Place broccoli and carrots into two separate shallow pans, arranging vegetables into a single layer. Drizzle the vegetables with a little coconut oil, using just enough to coat all the vegetables. Sprinkle with salt and pepper. Place vegetables in the oven and roast until slightly brown and tender. The carrots will take about 30 minutes. The broccoli will take only about 15 to 20. Remove and set aside.

▶ Prepare the phyllo. Don't open the phyllo package until you are ready to use it immediately. Melt the coconut oil and have the brush ready. Set the carrots and broccoli nearby. Lightly grease a large baking tray. As soon as you remove the phyllo from its package, cover it with enough plastic wrap so that none of the phyllo sheets are exposed. Then cover this with a damp kitchen towel.

▶ Each time you remove a phyllo sheet, re-cover the remaining stack with the plastic and damp towel so they don't dry out. Remove one sheet of phyllo and place it on a clean working surface, with the long side nearest you and brush lightly with melted coconut oil. Top with another phyllo sheet and brush with more oil. Cut oiled phyllo stack crosswise into 6 (roughly 12 by 2¾ inch) strips.

▶ Put a mixture of the carrots and broccoli near a corner of each strip on the end nearest you. Then fold corner of phyllo over to enclose the filling and form a triangle. Continue folding strip (like a flag), maintaining triangle shape. Put the triangle, seam-side down, on a large baking sheet lined with parchment paper and brush the top with a little coconut oil. Make remaining triangles in the same way.

▶ Bake the pillows in the middle of the oven until golden brown, 20 to 25 minutes, then transfer to a rack to cool slightly.

Suggestions

▶ Tracey's recipe calls for roasting the vegetables and brushing the phyllo sheets with olive oil, so if you prefer, use that instead of coconut oil.

Gluten-free ▲ Oil-free ▲ Easy
Total time: **90 minutes**

WHITE BEAN SALAD WITH CREAMY ITALIAN DRESSING

serves 4

Although it isn't heated, I include this in the Warm chapter because serving it at room temperature allows for all of the rich flavors to come through in each bite.

Salad

1 (15-ounce) can cannellini or great
    northern beans, rinsed and drained
1 (15-ounce) artichoke hearts, chopped
1 large carrot, peeled and chopped
1 large stalk celery, chopped
1 small zucchini, chopped
1 1/2 cups cherry tomatoes, left whole
1/2 cup fresh parsley, minced
1/4 cup chopped kalamata olives
2 Tbsp. sun-dried (not oil-packed)
    tomatoes, finely chopped
1 heaping Tbsp. chopped red onion
1 heaping Tbsp. capers, drained
1 tsp. dried thyme

Zest of 1 lemon
Ground black pepper, to taste
Fresh basil, for garnish, optional

Dressing

1/3 cup raw macadamia nuts or raw
    cashew pieces, soaked for 1 to 2
    hours, rinsed and drained
1/4 plus cup water
2 to 4 Tbsp. red wine vinegar
1 garlic clove
1 tsp. nutritional yeast
1/2 tsp. dried oregano
1/2 tsp. dried basil
Pinch sea salt

▶ In a large bowl, combine all of the salad ingredients (except for the basil), stir and set aside.
▶ In a high-speed or regular blender, combine all of the dressing ingredients and process until very smooth. Add more water if the dressing is too thick. Pour the dressing over the salad ingredients and stir to thoroughly combine. Garnish with fresh basil, if using.

Suggestions

▶ If your sun-dried tomatoes are particularly dry and hard, rehydrate them in hot water for about 10 minutes. Drain, pat dry, and mince.
▶ Serve this salad with Whole Wheat Pretzel Twists (see recipe on page 218), Raw Pesto Crackers (see recipe on page 182), on "Parmesan" Pita Chips (see recipe on page 180).

Gluten-free ▲ Oil-free ▲ Quick ▲ Easy

INGREDIENT & EQUIPMENT RESOURCES

I offer this short list of ingredient and equipment resources as a guide for the plant-based (or otherwise) cook. Just to get it on the table, with the exception of a few freebies here and there to sample and/or share with my blog readers, I am not affiliated with nor am I compensated by any of the companies listed below. These are simply the products and brands that I use in my own kitchen.

Amazon

Living out in the boonies means that I use Amazon A LOT. Seriously, they ought to send me some kind of commendation. I've ordered everything from food stuffs to kitchen items to clothing and shoes. If you can't find it on Amazon, it probably doesn't exist: Amazon.com.

Barnivore

Believe it or not, not all alcoholic beverages are vegan. Animal products may be used in the processing and filtering of beer, wine, and liquor—such as eggshells or fish bladder (yes, you read that correctly), more genteelly known as isinglass—or as ingredients, such as honey or even dairy. If you are 100% vegan and 100% plant-based, you want to avoid those drinks, but navigating the beverage aisle might be a little tricky. The website (and mobile app) Barnivore comes to the rescue with lists of wines and beers that are—and are not—vegan-friendly: Barnivore.com.

Bob's Red Mill

I get most of my rices, whole grains, gluten-free grains, coconut, and beans from Bob's. I appreciate their variety and quality: BobsRedMill.com.

Excalibur Dehydrators

What a noble but fitting name for a dehydrator! This is a big ticket item, but I use my 9-tray model to make oil-free raw crackers and cookies and for rising bread dough; you can make your own sugar-free dried fruit (and veggies) and fruit leathers too. Once you get into it, you'll be coming up with all kinds of things to dry out: ExcaliburDehydrator.com.

King Arthur Flour

The source for all things bread and baking. I love browsing through KAF's catalogue, daydreaming about all of the cool cooking equipment, ingredients, books, and utensils I know I must need. Beyond all those fun extravagances, KAF has wonderful flours and meals of all kinds: KingArthurFlour.com.

Lily's Sweets

I can't tell you how excited I was when I discovered Lily's Sweets chocolate chips. Why? They're stevia-sweetened! And they are delicious. They melt like a dream and have a rich, chocolate taste. Lily's has all kinds of other chocolate goodies, too: LilysSweets.com.

Living Tree Community

Proponents of "alive food," this online purveyor has a large assortment of products from nut butters, seeds, grains, spices, salts, sea vegetables, dried fruits and vegetables, chocolate, and even coffee: LivingTreeCommunity.com.

NuNaturals

I love NuNaturals stevia and other non-sugar sweeteners. This company is constantly coming up with amazing products such as their new chocolate sauce, simple syrup, and flavored stevias (think cherry, vanilla, and peppermint). Their stevia lacks that tell-tale bitter taste of most other stevia products: NuNaturals.com.

Richard's Maple Syrup

As it's located in the same county where I grew up, I've been enjoying Richard's beautiful, deep brown maple syrup for over 40 years. When I'm in Ohio visiting my parents, I'll often make a trip out to Chardon to pick up a half-gallon of syrup and a pound of maple sugar. Other brands just don't taste nearly as good, probably because Richard's have been making products with maple syrup since 1910 and know how to do it right: RichardsMapleProducts.com.

Source Naturals

This is the brand of organic spirulina that I buy to supplement smoothies and roll into energy bites and bars: SourceNaturals.com.

South River Miso Company

Based in Massachusetts, South River makes hand-crafted miso pastes using age-old Japanese methods. You'll find traditional soybean-based misos on their site, but also flavored misos and pastes made from azuki, barley, chickpea, and brown rice: SouthRiverMiso.com.

SunBiotics

The smell and flavor of SunBiotics Vanilla Probiotic Powder is warm and rich because it's enhanced with mesquite, yacon, and acacia gum fiber. I add a ½ teaspoon to my morning smoothie to keep those good GI flora thriving! SunBiotics also carries almonds, chocolate, and probiotic powders formulated for kids: SunBiotics.com.

Tinkyada Gluten-free Pastas

I am very pleased with the texture and flavor of Tinkyada's brown rice pastas, which come in all of the various shapes with which one is familiar. I use them in traditional pasta dishes as well as in vegan macaroni and cheez, and also in pasta salads: Tinkyada.com.

Todd's Seeds

For sprouting seeds, I go straight to Todd's. I've never had a fail with seeds from Todd's. That goes for wheatgrass, broccoli, radish, alfalfa, and other seeds I've purchased from him: ToddsSeeds.com.

Tofu Xpress

I love my tofu press and I use it several times a week. Tofu is like a super-saturated sponge when you break it out of its packaging. Pressing it removes that bland liquid so that you can replace it with highly-flavored, delicious marinades! If you're still using a stack of cookbooks to press your tofu, ask your significant other to buy you a real press for your birthday or Christmas: TofuXpress.com.

Vitamix

The prices will take your breath away, but I don't regret splurging on a high-speed blender. I use mine 3 to 4 times every day. It does creamy like nothing else. Look for less-expensive refurbished models on the Vitamix website: Vitamix.com.

COOKING MEASUREMENT EQUIVALENTS

Cups	Tablespoons	Fluid Ounces
⅛ cup	2 Tbsp.	1 fl. oz.
¼ cup	4 Tbsp.	2 fl. oz.
⅓ cup	5 Tbsp. + 1 tsp.	
½ cup	8 Tbsp.	4 fl. oz.
⅔ cup	10 Tbsp. + 2 tsp.	
¾ cup	12 Tbsp.	6 fl. oz.
1 cup	16 Tbsp.	8 fl. oz.

Cups	Fluid Ounces	Pints/Quarts/Gallons
1 cup	8 fl. oz.	½ pint
2 cups	16 fl. oz.	1 pint = ½ quart
3 cups	24 fl. oz.	1½ pints
4 cups	32 fl. oz.	2 pints = 1 quart
8 cups	64 fl. oz.	2 quarts = ½ gallon
16 cups	128 fl. oz.	4 quarts = 1 gallon

Other Helpful Equivalents

1 Tbsp.	3 tsp.
8 oz.	½ lb.
16 oz.	1 lb.

METRIC MEASUREMENT EQUIVALENTS

Approximate Weight Equivalents

Ounces	Pounds	Grams
4 oz.	¼ lb.	113 g
5 oz.		142 g
6 oz.		170 g
8 oz.	½ lb.	227 g
9 oz.		255 g
12 oz.	¾ lb.	340 g
16 oz.	1 lb.	454 g

Approximate Volume Equivalents

Cups	US Fluid Ounces	Milliliters
⅛ cup	1 fl. oz.	30 ml
¼ cup	2 fl. oz.	59 ml
½ cup	4 fl. oz.	118 ml
¾ cup	6 fl. oz.	177 ml
1 cup	8 fl. oz.	237 ml

Other Helpful Equivalents

½ tsp.	2½ ml
1 tsp.	5 ml
1 Tbsp.	15 ml

About Annie

ABOUT ANNIE

If there is an unnamed, undiagnosed condition where one suffers from planning, thinking about, and anticipating future breakfasts, lunches, and dinners while eating breakfast, lunch, or dinner, then I have it. And I don't want to be cured. But I wouldn't be opposed to having this ailment named after me.

I was fortunate to be raised in a home with two excellent cooks: my mom and dad. Mom covered the basics of breakfasts, lunches in brown paper bags, and a square meal at night. She also covered Thanksgiving and Easter dinners. Dad took over on Christmas Eve or whenever an ingredient—be it a stinky cheese or olives or eggplant or artichokes or polenta—caught his fancy. Sauce splatters and piles of pots and pans in the sink were guaranteed. Between mom and dad, my three siblings and I ate eclectically and well.

My own culinary journey got off to a rocky start when I began living on my own post-college. I went for convenience and speed (and sugary, fatty, salty) rather than quality. Slowly, however, I began buying more fresh and whole foods to make my own meals. At the same time, I was learning about what foods are best for our bodies. Long story short, my plodding and indirect journey led me to plant-based eating. I no longer rely on packaged, frozen, or prepared meals, and instead make everything we need right here in our own kitchen.

What about the non-food part of my life? Before escaping the mean city streets for the wild, windy plains of Oklahoma, I was an administrative assistant and office manager at a subscription fulfillment company in Boulder, at a think-tank in Santa Monica, at a university in Cambridge, MA, in the Green Zone in Baghdad, and at a non-profit in Washington, D.C.

I now spend a good deal of time walking the pastures trying to identify different types of grasses and insects, feeding hummingbirds, writing and reading, struggling to solve crossword puzzles (with a pen and a lot of Wite-Out), and blogging at *An Unrefined Vegan* and *Virtual Vegan Potluck*. I live in blissful satellite- and cable-free isolation with my husband, Kel, and our only son, Ike (part dachshund, part Labrador).

ACKNOWLEDGMENTS

Hannah Ballard, Acquisitions Editor at Cedar Fort Publishing, must be thanked first and foremost for finding me and my blog amongst the thousands of well-written, beautifully-photographed, and mouthwatering vegan food blogs out there. Hannah was nothing but kind, encouraging, enthusiastic, and supportive through the whole process. Justin Greer and Lauren Error took my words and photos and designed a beautiful book around them; I'm so appreciative of their efforts. And thanks be to Cedar Fort Publishing for giving this untested, unseasoned writer, photographer, and recipe-developer the opportunity to see her creations come to life in book form.

My handsome husband, Kel, deserves some kind of medal for his patience through the long months of creating and testing recipes—some that were triumphs and others that were total failures. He tasted them all and gave me the gentlest possible feedback. He's been my faithful and supportive partner every step of the way.

Speaking of taste-testing, this cookbook would not have been possible—or at least not as good—without the honest, inspirational, and constructive criticism of my recipe testers. It was so gratifying to have these wonderful strangers answer my call for help while I developed these recipes. They spent countless hours and dollars baking, dehydrating, stirring, and roasting—and, more than anything, blending—all in an effort to help me create the best recipes that I could. And they subtly (and not so subtly) let me know that I use too much vinegar and not enough salt. I want to specifically call out: Sara Christine, Dianne Wenz, Poppy Velosa, Diana Morrow, Mathilde Poulin, Maggie, Somer McCowan, Liezl, Alison, Sasha Itterman, Karen Scholl, Imelda, Jessica, and Teresa Rieland, who also proofread the manuscript before I handed it over to the publisher. Her suggestions and corrections were critical to the final book. Ladies, I'm grateful for your help.

The vegan community is a warm, supportive, and encouraging place with room at the table for all. As a relative latecomer to plant-based eating, I stand on the shoulders of giants—some of whom gave me and my book their stamp of approval. Thank you JL Fields, Nava Atlas, Kathy Hester, Robin Robertson, Julie Hasson, and Laura Theodore.

To the awe-inspiring Kathy Hester, Dianne Wenz, and Laura Theodore, whose support and encouragement have meant so much to me. They are the finest of mentors and they inspire me every day. A lifetime supply of Oklahoma pecans and virtual hugs to my pals Angela McKee and Poppy Velosa. "Love and guts" to Somer McCowan for being my biggest fan, sounding board, recipe tester, cheerleader, and Complaint Department, but most importantly for being my friend. In addition to being talented plant-based cooks, all six of these women are dedicated animal rights and plant-based activists.

A respectful nod to my fellow plant-based food and vegan bloggers who inspire me each and every day—just by doing what they do: making awesome food and loving the animals. Extra-special love to the women who shared their recipes here in this book. Their inclusion has made for a better final product. I must also mention all of those bloggers who have participated in any of the Virtual Vegan Potlucks held over the years. Thanks for partying with me.

Finally, with love and gratitude to my parents, who have nurtured and supported me with unconditional love. Pops, I always told you I was a late bloomer.

INDEX

REFERENCES

Books

Healing with Whole Foods: Asian Traditions and Modern Nutrition, 3rd Ed., by Paul Pitchford. North Atlantic Books (Publisher), 2002.

Herbal Medicine, Healing, and Cancer: A Comprehensive Program for Prevention and Treatment, by Donald R. Yance, Jr. CN, MH. Keats Publishing (Publisher), 1999.

Mary Bell's Complete Dehydrator Cookbook: Everything You Need To Know To Make Delicious Dried Snacks, Jerkies, Fruit Leathers, Nutritious Meals, and Even Potpourri, by Mary Bell. William Morrow (Publisher), 1994.

Prevent and Reverse Heart Disease: The Revolutionary, Scientifically Proven, Nutrition-Based Cure, by Caldwell B. Esselstyn, Jr., MD. Avery (Publisher), 2008.

Salt, Sugar, Fat: How the Food Giants Hooked Us, by Michael Moss. Random House (Publisher), 2013.

The China Study: The Most Comprehensive Study of Nutrition Ever Conducted and the Startling Implications for Diet, Weight-Loss, and Long-Term Health, by T. Colin Campbell, PhD., and Thomas M. Campbell II, MD. BenBella Books (Publisher), 2006.

The Raw Foods Resource Guide, by Jeremy Safron. Celestial Arts (Publisher), 2005.

Vegan Nutrition: A Survey of Research, by Gill Langley, MA, PhD. The Vegan Society, Ltd. (Publisher), 1991.

Websites

No Meat Athlete: Runs on Plants at NoMeatAthlete.com

Nutrition and You: Power Your Diet at http://www.nutrition-and-you.com

Organic Facts: Unbiased Information on Nutrition, Benefits of Food, and Home Remedies at OrganicFacts.net